MENTAL EXERCISE for DOGS

[2-in-1] A Family-Friendly Guide to Unleash Your Dog's Potential with Easy Step-by-Step Brain Games. Improve Your Bonds and Enjoy a Happy Life Together.

TIMI FOSTER

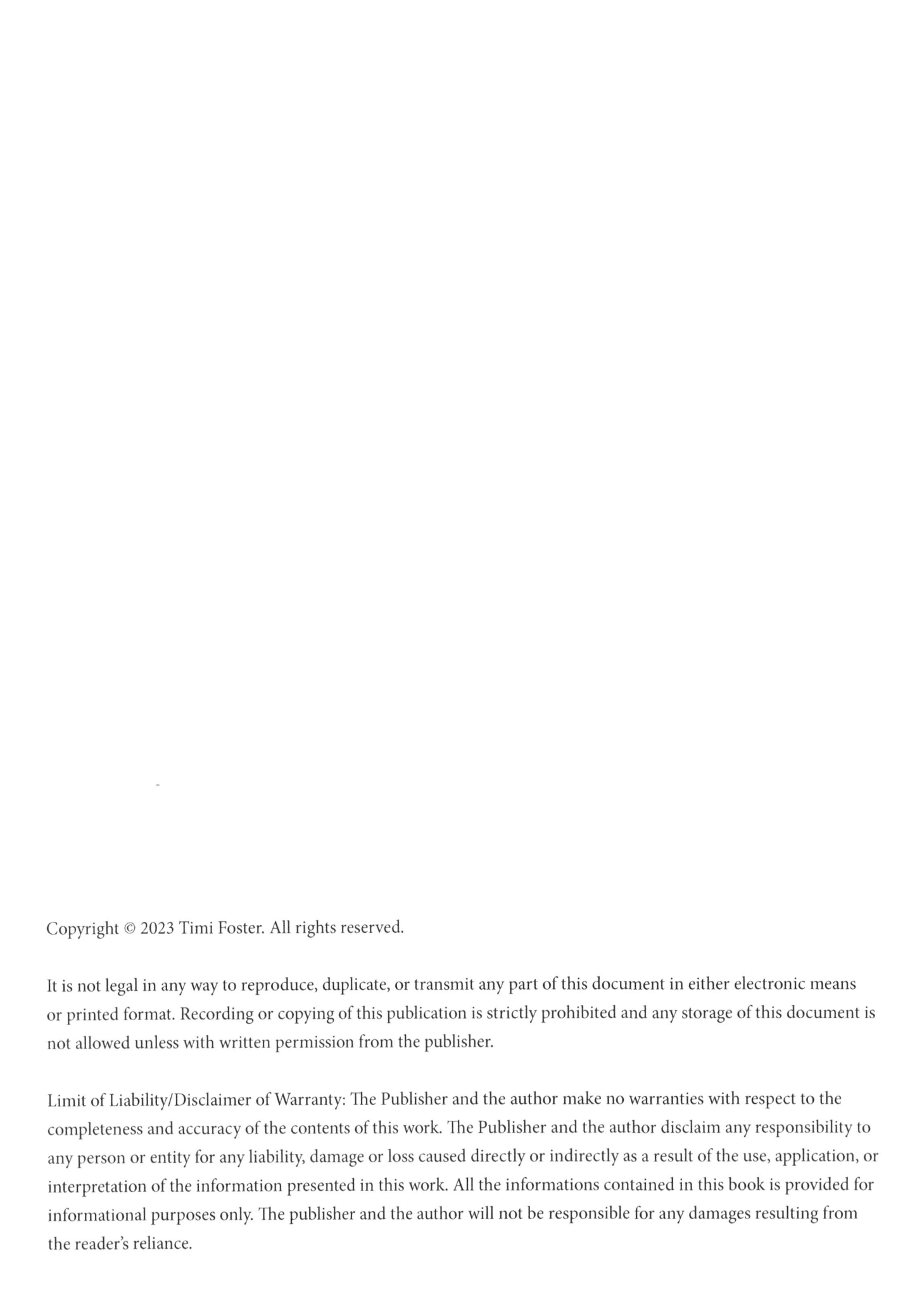

Copyright © 2023 Timi Foster. All rights reserved.

It is not legal in any way to reproduce, duplicate, or transmit any part of this document in either electronic means or printed format. Recording or copying of this publication is strictly prohibited and any storage of this document is not allowed unless with written permission from the publisher.

Limit of Liability/Disclaimer of Warranty: The Publisher and the author make no warranties with respect to the completeness and accuracy of the contents of this work. The Publisher and the author disclaim any responsibility to any person or entity for any liability, damage or loss caused directly or indirectly as a result of the use, application, or interpretation of the information presented in this work. All the informations contained in this book is provided for informational purposes only. The publisher and the author will not be responsible for any damages resulting from the reader's reliance.

BONUS

HOMEMADE HEALTHY DOG TREATS

Unleash the power of positive rinforcement

DOWNLOAD YOUR GIFT NOW

Navigate to the final page of the book and **SCAN** the **QR CODE** to download the **FREE BONUS**

Table of Contents

INTRODUCTION 7
   Book Structure 8

PART 1 - GUIDE SECTION 11

THE BENEFITS OF MENTAL TRAINING 12

Importance Of Mental Training for Dogs 12
Negative Conduct as A Result of Boredom and Ways to Prevent Them 13
How To Prevent Boredom in Dogs 15
Causes of stress and anxiety in dogs and how to prevent them 15
Tips and Best Practices to Grow a Strong and Unique Owner-Pet Relationship 16
A Trained Dog Is a Happy Dog 17
Conclusion 18

UNDERSTAND YOUR DOG 19

Simple Introduction to Canine Psychology and .. 19
Dog Memory 19
Canine psychology 19
Dog Memory 20
Recognizing different moods in dogs 20
   Happiness 21
   Fear 21
   Pain 22
   Nervousness 22
   Shyness 23
Canine communication 23
   Dog posture 24
   Barking 25
   Panting 26
   Chewing 26
   Eating unsuitable things 27
   Stealing 28
   Whining 28
   Digging 29
   Biting 29
Your Dog Needs 30
   Breed Characteristics 30
   Personalities 31
   Age and Life Stages 32
Conclusion 33

TRAINING ESSENTIALS FOR BEGINNERS 34

Essentials to Begin 34
How much time do you need to start a simple training routine? 35
Tips for establishing an effective training routine with your dog 35
Easy rules for carefree playing 36
The importance of involving all family members in training 37
Common Mistakes to avoid when training your dog 37
About Toys 38
   What to buy and how 38
   Surprise your dog with DIY toys 39
Conclusion 39

PART 2 - EXERCISE SECTION 40

MENTAL EXERCISE 42
BASIC LEVEL 42

   Sniff and Seek *43*
   Canine Castle *44*
   Toy Treasure Hunt *45*
   Tick Training Extravaganza *46*
   Puppy Party Games *47*
   Treat Towel Puzzle *48*
   Puzzle Feeder Frenzy *49*
   Bubble! Bubble!! Bubble!!! *51*
   Feather Frenzy *52*
   Eye Contact Mastery *53*
   Name Recognition Rally *54*
   Beam Balance Bliss *55*
   Snuffle Mat Challenge *56*
   Food Bowl Manners *57*
   Toy Take and Trade *58*
   Splash and Retrieve *59*
   Hidden Treats Hunt *60*
   Mind-Mazing Maze *61*
   Cardboard Treat Hunter *62*
   Treasure Box Sniffer *63*
   Mindfulness Moments *64*
   Cardboard Train *65*
   Solo Playtime Surprise *66*
   Stuffed Kong *67*
   Zen Zone Training *68*

MENTAL EXERCISE INTERMEDIATE LEVEL 69

Seek and Speak 70
The Which Hand Game 71
Spin the Bottle 72
Flying Disc Frenzy 74
Steady as a Rock 75
Teach and Show Off 76
Creative Trickster 77
Culinary Conundrum 78
Ball Pool Treasure Hunt 79
Sniff Puzzle Challenge 80
Jumping Jackpot 81
Tire Tango 82
Distracted Distinction 83
DIY Canine Obstacle Course 84
Frozen Goodies 85
The Blanket Race 86
Shell Game Challenge 87
Scavenger's Delight 88
Laundry Bin Treasure 89

MENTAL EXERCISE ADVANCED LEVEL 90

Musical Mat Challenge 91
Find Me Flip Me 92
Ultimate Trick Showcase 93
Hot & Cold 94
The Toys' Names 95
Discrimination Delight 96
Obstacle Course Masterpiece 97
Dog Helper 98
Discipline in Doggy Paradise 100
Three Cup Trick 101
Stability Ball Playtime 102
 Precision Target Training 103
Drawer Delight 104
Paws to Pedal 106
Scent Detective Training 107
Door Opener 108

A 30-day basic training program 110
A 30-day advanced training program 112

Bonus 115

INTRODUCTION

I'd like to welcome you into this entertaining yet educative journey with me. The objective of this book is to provide you with mentally engaging activities to promote a deeper connection between you and your dog, strengthen their cognitive abilities, and proffer solutions to behavioral problems our beautiful furry friends face through positive stimulation and fun activities for them.

This book was carefully crafted with the goal of all categories of dog owners in mind. So, it doesn't matter if this is your first time owning a pet dog or a dog lover. By the end of this book, you will have in your possession a comprehensive guide that makes mental training with your dog more accessible, enjoying and rewarding for you and your dog.

You don't have to take my word for it; take a peek at chapter 4 in the table of contents and see how many challenges and activities we will be covering over the course of this book.
While we are here, I'd like to give you a brief overview of this book. Your goals for picking up this book may vary from your neighbor's. However, the common goal we can all agree on at the end of this book includes these three:

1. To make mental training activities for dogs simple and accessible to everyone, even beginners.

For many of us dog owners, one of the mistakes we make concerning caring for our dogs is paying more attention to their physical well-being without paying any or very little attention to their mental health. In our defense, it's not the case that we don't care about our dogs' mental health; rather, we tend to focus on what we see, and that's evident even in how we conduct our day-to-day activities.
However, that doesn't have to be the case. While I'm positive that we all love and care for our dogs, showing love to these beautiful creatures goes beyond taking them for a walk in the park and giving them the best quality feed there is. One aspect of caring for our dogs we should never downplay is connecting with their minds. These could sometimes be daunting, especially when starting out at first.
For this purpose, I have taken quality time to demystify the concept of mental exercises for dogs through thoughtfully explained and broken-down instructions on how to go about them for all who consider their dog's mental health a necessity, regardless of their level of experience.

2. To make the experience of playing with one's pet enjoyable and an additional opportunity to strengthen the bond between owner and pet

At the core of every dog-human relationship lies a bond built on love and a series of activities and experiences that further strengthens this bond. Mentally engaging your dogs in certain activities are one of those shared experience between you and your dog that can deepen this bond.

As we know, dogs are not just social; they are also intelligent creatures. This means their minds thrive on challenges and interaction. The more you engage them in these activities and interactions, the smarter they become and respond to factors around them.

As you embark on mentally challenging activities with your dog, bearing in mind that there are levels to these challenges (and should be followed in subsequent levels of difficulty), you lay down a foundation for mutual growth, better communication, and cooperation between you and your dog.

3. To help dogs with behavioral problems solve them through intelligent play and positive stimulation.

Just as we have it with people with special needs, dogs also demand special care and attention due to behavioral issues. Thankfully, most of these challenges could be mitigated or resolved through some of the exercises we will see in this book.

Some of the few causes of these behavioral challenges include boredom, anxiety, or not meeting the needs of the dogs (intentionally or otherwise). However, when you make mental stimulation a part of their daily routine, you provide them with a way to put their energy into constructive use and build their focus.

This book dives deep into a plethora of mental training activities that tackle behavioral issues with dogs and offer a hands-on solution for problems associated with destructive chewing, excessive barking, and separation anxiety, to mention a few. Using intelligent play, and positive reinforcement, which you will pick up in the pages of this book, you will be able to empower your dog to outgrow these challenges, become more self-controlled, and even learn to groom more desirable behaviors.

BOOK STRUCTURE

This book is divided into two major categories: the guide section and the exercises section.

GUIDE SECTION

This section comprises three chapters to provide you with the basic knowledge and deeper understanding of why things are done in certain ways, assuming some of our readers will come from little to no experience handling dogs.

The outline of the chapters includes the following:

Chapter 1: All the Benefits of Mental Training for Your Dogs

Here, you get to learn about the following:

- Importance of mental training for dogs.
- Negative conduct as a result of boredom and preventing it.
- Causes of stress and anxiety in dogs and how to prevent them.
- Tips and best practices to grow a unique and strong owner-pet relationship.
- Why a trained dog is a happy dog.
- How to recognize signs of a lack of mental and physical stimulation.

Chapter 2: Understand Your Dog

In this chapter, we'll start by:

- Introducing you to the concepts of canine psychology and dog memory

Afterwards, we delve deep into the following concepts:

- Dog Observation, where you learn to recognize different dog moods such as fear, pain, playfulness, nervousness, boredom, shyness, etc. all by reading the dog's body language.
- Canine Communication: This entails dog postures, howling, barking, panting, chewing, eating unsuitable things, stealing, whining, digging, biting, etc.
- Identifying/understanding your dog's needs: Differences and preferences among different dog breeds, personalities, and specific needs related to age and life stages.

Chapter 3: Training Essentials for Beginners

In this chapter, we equip you with the essentials to begin. Here, we talk about:

- How much time you need to start a simple training (establishing a daily routine)
- Easy rules for carefree playing
- The importance of involving all family members in the training to facilitate achieving the result.
- Positive reinforcement: treats/food reinforcement and alternatives.

After these, we go into some of the common mistakes to avoid when dealing with our dogs. We discuss:

- No punishment (training with love and positive education)
- Frequent training mistakes
- Lastly, we round off the chapter by discussing toys, what to buy, letting your dog choose its toys, and simple DIY (Do It Yourself) examples with these toys.

EXERCISES SECTION

There's only so much that can be learned through theoretical knowledge. Hence, the reason for the latter section. With a solid theoretical foundation and tons of exercises, you are right on the path to creating a fulfilling chemistry between yourself and your beloved dog.

The practical section of this book is divided into three major categories:

- Basic
- Intermediate
- Advanced

This practical aspect of this book constitutes the larger portion as each category comprises about 25 to 30 exercises, as well as suggestions on where to perform them, toys, and other supporting tools.

We'll also dedicate a chapter under this section to shed more light on what I call the "**Training Program Planner**." This chapter was inspired by the idea similar to that of a cookbook that not only provides you with the recipes to prepare a dish but with the right amount and proportion, with detailed instructions. In the same way, after providing you with tons of activities of different levels, it's only right to consolidate them all into a plan to leave you with something you can work with or, better still, modify to your and your dog's preference with all the knowledge garnered from this book.

This chapter is divided into two categories, namely:

- A 30-day basic training program
- A 30-day advanced training program

DISCLAIMER

It is important to note that not all dogs will enjoy the same activities, and some may have preferences, so it's important to experiment with different activities to find what your dog likes.

As always, it is important to consult with a veterinarian before starting any new activities with your dog, especially if they have any health issues.

NOTE

Throughout this book, you'll find that I refer to dog using third-person pronoun "him." Animals are generally referred to as "it," but in our case, I want to assume are our dogs are precious to us, and as such, it is okay to refer to them as "he" or "her" as the case may be.

However, the contents of this book are not gender-specific as the word "him" was chosen only to remain consistent in how I refer to dogs in a sentence.

As you can see, this book is value-packed to prepare you for the journey of transforming your relationship with your dog by building stronger connections, fostering cognitive growth, and building desirable behaviors.

I look forward to walking every step with you as we unlock the full potential of these lovely creatures' mental capacity and build a partnership/relationship that brings happiness and fulfillment to you, your family, and your dog's lives.

PART 1 - GUIDE SECTION

Dogs, just like us humans, need mental stimulation to always be at their best. It's a fact that mental training for dogs is commonly overlooked while physical training is prioritized. Sometimes, we don't see the need to practice these mentally-stimulating exercises with our dogs until we begin to notice a change in how they behave.

Some of us could be lucky to detect these changes early, while others may not be so lucky. In either case, even if we don't doubt our love and care for these wonderful creatures, it could simply be negligence on our part or not being privy to the benefits of training your dog mentally. Also, there's no better way to start this book than to fill your mind with the many benefits that transcend both worlds when you make it a habit to improve your dog's mental abilities.

CHAPTER 1
THE BENEFITS OF MENTAL TRAINING FOR YOUR DOGS

IMPORTANCE OF MENTAL TRAINING FOR DOGS

Working with your dog to improve their cognitive function does more than just keep them busy. Below are some of the benefits your dog gets to enjoy when you mentally stimulate them regularly:

1. Helps alleviate boredom. One of the greatest side effects of not mentally engaging your dogs is boredom. While we are at school or at work, engaging in mentally challenging activities, our dogs are left alone at home for many hours. Without the right guidance and preparation, this may result in boredom. And trust me, dogs act quite strangely than us humans when they are bored. Boredom in dogs often leads to undesirable activities like scratching up furniture, chewing on things, barking excessively, or digging up plants.
Mental stimulation can help your dog get used to socializing with other pets (if any) or children at home. It's impossible to put aside our responsibilities at work and school to always be with our dogs, but we always need to be conscious of our responsibilities as dog owners by providing them with sufficient exercise and mental stimulation so that they are less bored and even less likely to exhibit any of those weird behaviors.

2. It helps them stay sharp. Even as humans, when we do everything but neglect our mental health, it tends to slow us down; we assimilate things longer than we should and even possibly cause premature aging. It's pretty much the same with dogs. It's even more tragic for our dogs since they have a much shorter lifespan compared to us. Mentally stimulating your dog not only keeps them sharp as they age, but it also helps combat symptoms of mental issues such as dementia, depression, or anxiety. Most importantly, a mentally trained dog breeds smart and happy puppies.

3. It is necessary for your dog's happiness. Mental stimulation can be very helpful in fighting off depression in dogs and keeping them happy. Depending on your dog breed, working dogs are usually very active and may require way more stimulation than other breeds. However, it is important that you incorporate mental training into your dog's life if you truly want to be invested in their happiness in the long run.

4. Reduces hyperactivity in dogs. Dogs are creatures filled with bursts of energy, and there's only so much they can do on their own. If you leave your dog at home all day with nothing to indulge them, they become hyperactive, which may start as them just constituting a nuisance to the house before it escalates into a more severe issue.
Dogs' energy level varies according to their breeds, age, and health. However, getting your dog to work off that energy in both physically and mentally engaging activities has been scientifically proven to lessen their hyperactivity and keep them calm.

5. It's a workout for the brain. Physical activities are good for preventing your dog's muscles from getting weak, just the same way daily stimulation of your dog's brain will prevent him from aging prematurely. Dogs that haven't been mentally stimulated for a major part of their lives are more prone to cognitive dysfunction as they age. As we will see in chapter four, there are tons of interactive treats and puzzles you can engage your dog with that will prove very helpful in making them mentally active and responsive throughout their lives.

6. Good Habits for Young Pups. Physical and mental stimulation are essential for dogs in their early years. Study shows that it teaches them to develop good habits, become more confident and help them put their energy to constructive use.

NEGATIVE CONDUCT AS A RESULT OF BOREDOM AND WAYS TO PREVENT THEM

Have you found yourself in a situation where you come back home to a piece of shredded furniture or toilet paper unrolled or torn all over the place? And then you look at your dog, and he greets you wagging his tail? Well, it's not the case. Your dog is badly behaved, as it might seem. It might simply be a case of dog boredom.

If you own a dog, you should know that as social creatures, dogs will create their own fun. And most times, in ways that don't sit well with us. When left at the mercy of their judgment, dogs will shred pillows, chew furniture, and do whatever they can to pass the time. And it's all the more exciting for them because you're not there to stop them.

When you begin to notice big messes whenever you get back home-tripping over trash cans, digging dirt in the backyard-it's a clear indication of boredom in your dog. You can also tell these signs even when you're at home with them. If your dog is always acting restless around or mugging you for attention, he's most likely bored and needs you to engage him in something fun.

Studies show that animals, just like humans, can become bored and develop signs of anxiety or depression if left unstimulated for long periods. Below are some warning signs to look out for to prevent the long-term effects of boredom on your beautiful pet:

1. Damaging Furniture. If you notice your pet acting out and tearing up your furniture, constantly chewing on your coffee table legs, or being destructive in areas around the house where they'd normally avoid, it's one of the early effects of boredom which you should take seriously.

2. Repetitive Behaviors. Dogs, too, can develop impulsive actions, usually as a side effect of boredom, stress, or anxiety.

Repetitive behaviors are a form of pet obsessive-compulsive disorder, and you should be particularly mindful when you begin to notice these signs in your pet:

- Tail chasing
- Pacing
- Shadow or light chasing
- Spinning
- Excessive scratching, licking or biting

Some of these behaviors could be harmful to the dogs and even the people at home. Ensure you consult a veterinarian as soon as you start noticing these signs.

3. A sudden change in bathroom behaviors. To some dogs, boredom could cause them to poop or pee in places other than their potty spots. If you notice your well-trained pet is suddenly defecating in unusual places in the house, it could be a sign of boredom or trying to get revenge on you for leaving them idle for long periods of time.

However, you want to be sure that all other possibilities, such as your bet being pregnant, nursing, or still in the pup age, are ruled out before taking steps to prevent such events from happening again.

4. Fighting with other pets. As I mentioned earlier, dogs will do what they can to create their own fun. When your dog is bored, he'll look for something entertaining, even if that implies stepping on the toes of other pets in the house. When you begin to notice your dog getting aggressive with other pets that they would otherwise be cordial with, it's a sign that you're not giving him enough mental stimulation to keep his calm. Now, don't get me wrong! Pets play fight for fun. However, you can tell when the fighting has turned serious through the following signs:

- Physically harming other pets
- Stiff tail or gaze
- Excessive chasing or corning other pets
- Excessive barking

Separate the pets immediately if you notice any of the following to prevent things from getting further out of hand.

HOW TO PREVENT BOREDOM IN DOGS

When our dogs can't find ways to engage their natural instincts to play or think, they become restless, which often leads to anxiety and depression. There are different ways to solve this problem on a general level, some of which include the following:

- Ensure there are plenty of toys around for your dog to play with. In a later chapter, we'll talk about how your dogs can select the toys they love the most.
- Treat your pets to low-calorie feeds that are rich in protein to give them the fuel they need to play without making them feel heavy.
- Find ways to keep your dog busy at home using activity posts and guilty obstacles.
- Increase their playtime. Your dog may not be getting enough playtime which could be the reason why it is acting up. Increasing their playtime, even as little as an extra ten minutes, could make all the difference.

CAUSES OF STRESS AND ANXIETY IN DOGS AND HOW TO PREVENT THEM

As humans, we're probably familiar with how our body responds to stress and how to de-stress. But how do you know your dog is stressed out? Are there tell signs to indicate that these creatures are acting under the influence of stress and anxiety?

As a pet parent, you are the closest person to helping your dog defeat stress. Hence, it is important that you're able to identify when they are stressed and how to get them to relax.

Below are some of the major causes of stress in dogs:

- **Fear:** This could be as a result of one of the following:

  - Extremely loud noises: Dogs have a very sensitive sense of hearing. This implies that an average noise to us humans would be amplified to them. These very loud noises may make them uncomfortable, increase their stress levels, and may result in them acting differently.

  - Change of environment: This is often associated with moving to a new house, rehoming a dog after the passing of a loved one, or bringing a newly adopted dog home for the first time. What may seem to us as the dog acting out might just be the dog's reaction to responding to stress and anxiety.
- **Memory loss and confusion** (often associated with aging)
- **Separation**

Also, a recent study, according to www.nature.com, shows that the emotional health and stress levels of dog owners can also impact the dog's stress level. Hence, it has been shown that dogs can, to a good extent, mirror the stress levels of their owners.

Additionally, it's not uncommon for stressed dogs to show similar signs as they would when bored, some of which include:

- Repetitive behavior
- Sudden aggression
- Pacing/restlessness
- Panting
- Destroying objects at home

If you notice any of these behaviors in your dog, the first thing to do is consider the nature and personality of your dog. Also, you want to be sure your emotional state is in order. Next, you may want to speak to the veterinarian if there's no progress. The last thing you want to do is scold your pet at this stage. As we progress, we'll see why scolding your dog would do more harm than good.

TIPS AND BEST PRACTICES TO GROW A STRONG AND UNIQUE OWNER-PET RELATIONSHIP

If your dog is always happy around you, it's a sign of good bonding between the both of you. You wouldn't want your dog acting all fearful- ears back, tail down and running off- when you're around.

On the other hand, you also would not want your dog to exhibit traits of separation anxiety, where they can't let you step out of the house for a minute. That's somewhat of an unhealthy attachment.

What you want is a happy dog who is not always clingy. Forming a good bond with your dog doesn't necessarily imply spending the whole day together. There are a variety of ways to achieve this; let's take a look at some of the most ways to get this done:

1. Ensure consistency in how you communicate. It's possible for you to love your dog and vice-versa, but that doesn't automatically translate into forming the strongest of bonds. Inconsistency in how you communicate with your dog is one of the biggest challenges that must be addressed if you want to build a stronger bond with your dog. For instance, your dog sees a stranger coming towards you- even if it's a friend- and reacts by barking. And that's fine. However, how you caution it to stop barking when it sees a friend is important. You want to be consistent in whatever way you choose to tell it to stop barking when it sees you with certain people. You wouldn't want to be sending your mixed signals by communicating with it differently whenever it sees you with someone.

2. Provide comfort to your dog. There's a wrong perception that dogs become more fearful when their pet parents comfort them when they are scared. That's absolutely not true! It's the same as saying petting and hugging a crying baby will make it cry all the more. It's impossible to create fear by showing love to your dog. So, go ahead and show your dog all the love and care you can when you notice it being scared.

3. Find out what your pet likes. Let me let you in on one truth: Not all dogs enjoy walking in the park or playing the good-ol-fetch game. Personalities of dogs vary from individual and breed. Hence, it's up to you to study your pet to know their preferences and see what really gets him excited. One of the biggest red flags in building a bond with your dog is forcing it to do things he doesn't want to do. If you decide to keep taking your dog out for walks without taking into consideration whether he is scared of being around strangers, or loud noise, this could affect your relationship, even though you might be doing it from a place of love.

4. Teach your dog new things. One of the best ways to strengthen the bond between you and your pooch is through positive reinforcement, training-trying out new things together. When you and your dog engage in new activities together, it helps your dog understand how to act and react to you in different cases. For instance, you could reward your dog by giving him a treat- a new toy or throwing the ball- whenever he adheres to your teaching. Activities like these are particularly helpful, especially when trying to teach your dog canine sports, such as agility training.

5. Learn canine body language. I'm sure you're aware that a dog wags its tail when it is happy. But do you know it also wags its tail when it is nervous? Just like us, dogs can communicate with their entire bodies. Hence, you have to be familiar with their body language if you want to really understand how they're feeling. This helps you tap into their emotions and, in the process, takes your bond to the next level. Don't worry if you don't know much about canine language for now; we will be addressing it in the next chapter.

6. Dogs need their own space, too! Don't take it personally when your dog needs his space. You have to understand that not all dogs are social in the same way. While some are naturally social, others are more reserved by nature. Factors such as dog personality and breed are also to be taken into consideration in situations like this. So, when your dog decides to take his nap in the next room, leave him be! It's not that deep!

A TRAINED DOG IS A HAPPY DOG

Training your dog might not be the easiest thing to do, but one that is worth it. You'll grow to love your dog for it once you begin to see the effects of this training- both physically and mentally- in how they act.

From experience, I can tell you the most submissive and aggressive dogs are as a result of a lack of structure both in terms of physical and mental training in the dog's life. A trained dog is more reliable, needs fewer restrictions, and is more confident.

Training helps to strengthen the bond between you and your dog, builds respect, and improves how you communicate. Training your dog also benefits you in the long run because you'll not only be helping him become more responsive, it puts you in a position to control his behavior in emergency cases, which could save his life.

Without proper training, dogs tend to misbehave, and when a dog begins to misbehave, you're not the only one that suffers- everyone around you, too! You, because the dogs live with you, and others because the dog begins to constitute a nuisance wherever it goes.

A well-trained dog is a pleasure to own because we won't have to worry about it being a risk to others. Besides, we all want a dog that can show off good manners in the crowd when we have guests at home and is reliable with kids around the house. As you can see, a well-behaved dog benefits everyone but doesn't come without the right training.

How to recognize signs of a lack of mental and physical stimulation.

To encapsulate all that we have said so far about mental and physical stimulation in dogs, below are signs you should look out for as quickly as possible:

- Destroying things
- Tail chasing
- Irregular barking
- Restlessness
- Excessive sleeping
- Digging
- Whining
- Stiffness
- Overeating
- Being withdrawn

CONCLUSION

Before we wrap up this chapter, note that there is no one-size-fits-all kind of training for all dogs. And that's why we have up to 50 different mental training exercises to try out with your dog. As we continue with this book, I want you to feel encouraged every step of the way because it will pay off in the end. Also, you wouldn't want your moodiness to rub off on your dog, as that would defeat the purpose of getting this book in the first place.

CHAPTER 2
UNDERSTAND YOUR DOG

In the last chapter, we discussed the benefits of mental training for your dog, causes and signs of boredom, and behaviors to look out for in recognizing a lack of mental and physical stimulation. It is vital that we have a good background on the importance of mental training to set the pace for subsequent chapters. In this chapter, we will be channeling our energy to something more intimate for the mutual benefit of you and your dog.

Watching Scooby-doo as a cartoon was fun, but have you ever wondered what it would look like if we could communicate verbally with our dogs? Wouldn't it be nice to know how their voice sounds other than barking and the sounds we're now used to? While it may not be entirely possible to communicate with our dogs verbally, fortunately, there is another way we can effectively communicate with them—and it all begins with understanding our dogs.

Once you understand your dog's body language, it's almost as good as your dog talking to you. To effectively kick off this chapter, I'd like to introduce the concepts of canine psychology and dog memory, as they both play an important role in understanding our dogs.

SIMPLE INTRODUCTION TO CANINE PSYCHOLOGY AND DOG MEMORY

Canine psychology and dog memory are two interesting fields in the study of dogs that offer us valuable insights as to how we interact with our dogs and vice-versa. Understanding how our lovely pets think helps strengthen our connection with them, tackle their behavioral challenges and help them lead a better life.

CANINE PSYCHOLOGY

According to the English dictionary, the term psychology refers to the study of mind and behavior or the mental or behavioral characteristics of an individual or group. From this context, we can define canine psychology as the study of the behavior of dogs, their emotions, as well as their cognitive responses.

We are fully aware of the various emotions-happiness, fear, anger, sadness, and affection- our dogs possess. In addition, we also know that our dogs' personality varies, just the same as their learning abilities and social behaviors. The concept of canine psychology is vital in helping us understand the reason why our dogs act in certain ways and develop training techniques that match the personality of our dogs.

DOG MEMORY

There are many fascinating features about a dog, but one that is of interest to dog researchers and enthusiasts is a dog's memory. It was believed that dogs have a relatively short memory compared to their pet parent species. However, further research proves that dogs have extended memory capabilities beyond their short-term memory.

While dogs have a great short-term memory that enables them to recall events for a short period, dogs have a recommendable associative memory that enables them to act and respond to commands, recognize faces, and complete tasks.

In addition to short-term and associative memory, dogs possess spatial memory that enables them to recollect recognizable environments. Their spatial memory is responsible for helping them remember their favorite food, toys, resting areas, potty spots, toys, etc. In other cases and breeds, this spatial memory helps them to recognize boundaries and territories among other dogs.

As you can see, dogs have a large memory, by extension, and it would be a waste of traits if we don't train our dogs to put them to effective use. Now, the concepts of canine psychology and dog memory could be complex, and I don't expect the average dog owner to have a degree in these areas to have a great bond with their dog.

As we proceed in this chapter, we will address some of the factors that help us understand the power of dog psychology and appreciate the various signs and body language we can use to enhance our relationship with our dogs.

RECOGNIZING DIFFERENT MOODS IN DOGS

All pet owners, at some point, must have wondered, "What is my dog thinking?" It's normal, especially as a new pet parent. While some may be able to recognize their dog's mood by merely spending time with them, not everyone has the luxury of time to spare.

As humans, we rely primarily on languages for communication. On the other hand, dogs tell us a lot about their emotional state based on their body language. Hence, it is always a good idea to understand how to communicate and recognize your dog's mood by merely observing his body language.

Let's take a look at some of the common body languages of dogs that represent different moods:

Note: Context is key when it comes to observing the body language of dogs. It's not uncommon for dogs to show a particular sign for more than one mood. So, as you pay attention to their body language, you also want to consider external factors that could play a role in how your dog is acting or responding.

HAPPINESS

This is usually not a tough nut to crack, as we've seen them often in our dogs or other dogs. You can identify a happy through the following signs:

- **Relaxed Posture.** A happy dog usually assumes a relaxed posture with smooth hair. In addition to his posture, his mouth is open and relaxed, ears in a natural position, and eyes in a normal shape are clear signs of happiness in your dog.
- **Playful Mood.** You can tell a dog is in the mood for some fun when his front end is lowered and rear end raised, with a high wagging tail and smooth hair. These body language signals are often accompanied by excited barking, and their eyes and ears are in their normal shape and position.

In addition to these, if you notice your dog's weight evenly distributed across his four paws, his hair is smooth, his face is looking interested, his mouth is open, and his tail is wagging, they are good indications that your dog is in a happy mood and ready to rock and roll with you.

Other common body languages of a happy dog include the following:

- **Wagging tail:** While this may vary depending on your dog's breed and personality, a loose and wagging tail is a clear indication of happiness.
- **Relaxed eyes:** A happy dog has relaxed and bright eyes, indicating no sign of worry or anxiety.
- **Soft ears:** This, too, may vary from breed to breed. For some, their ears could be perked up, while others may have their ears relaxed when happy. Conventionally, their ears should be in their natural position- not flattened against the head, or pinned back, as that would translate to a different meaning.
- **Body wiggle:** It's common for dogs to wiggle their body as a show of excitement and enthusiasm.

FEAR

Dogs do a great job of communicating their fear and distress through their body language. Obvious signs to look out for include trembling, crouching, and ears to the back. Bearing in mind that fear responses may vary from dog to dog, common body languages associated with fear in dogs include the following:

- **Ears pinned to the back:** As opposed to his happy mood when his ears are in a natural position, if you notice your dog's ear pinned to the back, together with one or more of the other signs we'll be discussing here, that's your dog telling you it's scared.
- **Playful Mood.** You can tell a dog is in the mood for some fun when his front end is lowered and rear end raised, with a high wagging tail and smooth hair. These body language signals are often accompanied by excited barking, and their eyes and ears are in their normal shape and position.
- **Excessive panting:** When dogs begin to act restless, it's a way of expressing fear of a situation and trying to escape such a situation. In some cases, they tend to seek safety and security by hiding behind objects.

- **Tails tucked beneath the abdomen:** Several moods cause a dog to tuck his tail between his legs. This includes stress, fear, or being unsure of what to do. However, if you notice your dog has its tail tucked beneath its abdomen, that's your dog screaming "I'm frightened!", "Please don't hurt me!"
- **Aggression or defensive behavior:** Body languages that portray these behaviors include barking, growling, or snarling. A dog becomes defensively aggressive towards a person or another dog it sees as a threat and cannot escape the perceived risk.
- **Lip licking or yawning:** When your dog begins to lick his lip, yawns, or salivates for no obvious physical reason, such as exercise, heat, presence of food, or tiredness, chances are your dog is scared. In this case, it is necessary to observe your environment to determine if he's perceiving a threat that's making him act in such a manner.

PAIN

Not many people know this, but dogs are very good at hiding signs of pain when they're outside, which is a means of their survival tactics. However, they tend to be more vulnerable with their owners by showing pain through their body language. With the right understanding of your dog's personality and keeping an eye out for certain behaviors, you can rest assured that you'll notice how your dog communicates this feeling to you. Common body languages dog exhibit to show pain include:

- **Vocalization:** Take note of the sounds your dog makes when touched or move in a certain way. This may include whining, growling, or yelping, especially when done more than usual.
- **Altered gait:** Dogs in pain are likely to have challenges moving around, standing up or lying down. As a result, they tend to favor one limb over the other, which affects their posture.
- **Restlessness:** Fear is not the only mood that can cause your dog to be restless. When dogs find it difficult to maintain their composure, it could be an underlying cause of pain.
- **Dilated pupils:** This indicates discomfort caused by pain or distress.
- **Excessive/abnormal licking or biting:** If your dog repeatedly licks or bites a certain part of his body, he could be doing this to ease the pain or draw your attention to the area of discomfort.
- **Hunched posture:** Back arching in dogs is often linked to gastrointestinal pain or spinal discomfort. You know your dog is in distress when you see it having a hunched posture that is accompanied by walking off balance, panting, or shaking.

NERVOUSNESS

Dogs experience and express nervousness and anxiety in their unique ways. Keeping a close eye on your dog's body language can provide valuable insights into his emotions. There are certain cues to recognize nervousness in dogs, some of which include the following:

- **Tucked Tail:** A dog's tail says a lot about him. A tucked tail doesn't always translate to fright. Your dog would also tuck his tail when he's being defensive, nervous, and in pain. While this is a clear indicator of attention, you also want to pay attention to the other behaviors he shows to be certain of what he's trying to tell you.
- **Pulled back ears:** Just as you can tell a dog is happy when he's wagging his tail, pulled back ears or ears flattened against the head is an obvious body language used by dogs to communicate nervousness.

- **Hypervigilant:** When you notice your dog pacing around and looking in all directions, he's most likely nervous and scanning for threats around him or the house. You also want to pay close attention when he accompanies these signs with barking or whining.
- **Lip licking:** Once your dog begins to lick his lip or yawn without anything appetizing around, you want to pay close attention to him as well as the other cues in this category as a sign of nervousness.
- **Excessive shedding:** This may be caused by a variety of reasons-low quality food, incompatible shampoo, parasites, anxiety, or maybe other underlying issues. Try talking to your vet to be sure of the cause of your dog's shedding.
- **Avoiding eye contact:** It is not uncommon for dogs that have been rescued from traumatic situations to avoid eye contact. However, if that's not the case with yours, it's an indicator of the signal of anxiety, especially when accompanied by whining and pacing.
- **Furrowed brow:** Just as a happy dog has a relaxed face and soft eyes, an anxious or nervous dog communicates this mood with a furrowed brow and tight facial muscles.

SHYNESS

As we know, dogs have various personalities - some are approachable, independent, and playful - and one of these personalities is shyness. In addition to their inherent personalities, other factors that can trigger shyness in dogs include being around strangers or unfamiliar dogs, which can cause them to act shy. Shyness in dogs could come in different contexts, such as social shyness, sound sensitivities, or even fear contexts. Hence, they may tend to exhibit common signs such as the following:

- **Tail tucking**
- **Hunching/cowering**
- **Avoiding eye contact**
- **Ears pulled back**
- **Submissive behavior**
- **Slow movements**

Again, it is important to read the environment, not to interpret what he's trying to tell you for something else.

CANINE COMMUNICATION

Canine communication refers to the various ways a dog communicates with humans as well as other dogs. This includes the use of their senses, body postures, and vocalizations such as barking, growling, whining, etc. We've seen how a dog communicates their moods through various body languages. As we progress, we'll continue to see how body postures and olfactory cues play a significant role in dog communication.

One major difference between humans and dogs is that while humans are listeners, dogs are watchers. Hence, vocal communications are much less significant to them than the use of body language and posturing, including the position of their heads, necks, tails, ears, etc.

People who desire to understand their dogs better should pay attention to the way they communicate because, as we have seen from their body language, it's possible for dogs to exhibit body languages that are quite conflicting for different moods.

We'll now explore the various ways dogs communicate through the following:

- **Dog postures**
- **Barking**
- **Panting**
- **Chewing**
- **Eating unsuitable things**
- **Stealing**
- **Whining**
- **Digging**
- **Biting**

DOG POSTURE

There are various ways a dog uses his posture to communicate his mood, intentions, and social status. Some of these postures include the following:

- **Relaxed Body:** A relaxed posture is usually accompanied by a neutral face and loose muscles. It indicates that your dog is at ease and comfortable in his surroundings.
- **Submissive/Fearful Posture:** A dog assumes a submissive posture when trying to appease a dominant individual or dog. Postures include rolling on their back to show their belly, avoiding eye contact, lowering their heads, crouching to the ground, and tucking their tails between their legs.
- **Tense Body:** A tense or stiff body is often a means of communicating alertness or anxiety. This posture is followed by a rigid body, stiff face, mouth tightly closed, hair on the back and a focused gaze. A dog in this position may be in the face of a threat and trying to react defensively to the situation.
- **Play Bow:** The play bow position is often the most common posture dogs use to communicate during play time. The dog assumes this posture by lowering its front end, while raising its rear end, usually accompanied by its wagging tail. You know it's game time, especially when your dog keeps bouncing in this position.
- **Aggressive Posture:** A dog that displays an aggressive posture does this with the intention to intimidate, threaten, and cause harm. Such posture is demonstrated by the dog standing upright, intense stare, baring teeth, and growling/snarling. In some cases, the dog could have its ears positioned forward, signaling its readiness to fight.
- **Dominant Posture:** This posture is usually communicated between dogs to assert their dominance over other dogs. They assume an upright stance, with their tail facing upwards and an eye-to-eye contact. In some cases, the dominant dog places his paw on objects or other dogs as a means to claim dominance.

As a dog owner, it is vital that you're able to identify these postures in your dog and be able to decipher what he's trying to tell you in that situation. To do this effectively, you should be able to combine these canine body postures, their body language and the environmental context to tell your dog's mood and intentions.

BARKING

Barking is one of the common means of vocalization in dogs. Not expecting a dog to bark is as unreasonable as not wanting a child to cry or talk. However, some dogs may quickly become a nuisance by barking excessively. If that's the case, you want to find out the cause of their excessive barking. Once you figure out the cause, it becomes easier to fix the excessive barking issue.

Barking could represent different things according to the environmental context of the dog. Below are some of the messages dogs pass through their barking:

- **Territorial Defense.** Dogs are territorial by nature. Hence, it's normal for them to assert aggression in the face of a threat to protect their territory. When the perceived threat (person or another dog) comes closer to your territory, the bark gets louder and assumes his aggressive posture, and is ready to strike if need be.
- **Fear or Alarm.** Dogs also bark when they get startled by something strange or if something catches their attention, and this could happen anywhere. Barking accompanied by their ears in the back position and tails tucked are common signs of fear in dogs.
- **Boredom.** As pack animals, when left alone for long periods, dogs may begin to bark. This is often as a result of boredom, loneliness, or sadness.
- **Excitement.** Dogs bark as a sign of greeting people or other animals. You can tell it's a happy bark when its tail wags and bounces around, accompanying it. They may also bark to express their enthusiasm for engaging in playful activities.
- **Attention Seeking.** Dogs may bark (somewhat repetitively) when they need to get the attention of their owners or the people around them. For instance, a dog barks when he wants to be fed, played with, or let outside.
- **Separation Anxiety/Compulsive Barking.** Separation anxiety could be the reason why a dog barks excessively. Dogs with this issue tend to exhibit other symptoms, such as pacing, inappropriate elimination, destructiveness, and depression. On the other hand, compulsive barkers would bark for anyone who cares to hear the sound of their voices, usually accompanied by running around a fence or in circles. contact. In some cases, the dominant dog places his paw on objects or other dogs as a means to claim dominance.

Not to sound like a broken record, but context is key! Pay attention to the context- barking tone, pitch, and duration- as well as your dog's behaviors when trying to interpret his barking. Having a good grasp of these will promote good communication between you and your dog and help you better understand his needs.

PANTING

Dogs were not created with sweat glands, but there must be a way to regulate their body temperature- thermoregulation- and this is achieved through panting. However, panting in dogs could also mean different things depending on other factors, such as their behaviors and the context.

Below are some messages dogs convey through panting:

- **Thermoregulation.** In the absence of sweat glands, dogs pant to cool off when they're hot. When the temperature is heated up, and the dog is feeling really hot, he goes to a cool place to lie down, where he can absorb cooler air from the surroundings.
The inhaled air gets to his upper respiratory system and, in the process, evaporates water from his tongue and mucous membranes. Afterwards, he drinks a lot of water to compensate for the evaporation losses. This is an important mechanism in dogs since they are most likely to feel the effect of heat exhaustion.
- **Stress and Anxiety.** Panting could also be a psychological response to threat, anxiety, or fear. Other behaviors that accompany this message include restlessness, pacing, trembling.
- **Excitement.** Your dog expresses his excitement or anticipation for meeting someone (a familiar face approaching him), going for a walk, or meeting other dogs. You can easily tell he's eagerly waiting for something exciting when he pants while wagging his tail.
- **Pain.** Dogs could be quickly misunderstood when we don't know what to look out for in different situations. A dog would pant for excitement and would do the same when feeling pain or discomfort. However, when you pay attention to other accompanying cues such as whining, limping, sudden change in appetite, and overall negative demeanor, you can be sure it's time to consult your vet.
- **Physical exercise.** Panting after a strenuous activity helps restore dogs to their normal breathing pattern by increasing oxygen flow to their lungs. So, you should expect similar behavior for your dog, just as your body would react after jogging three laps of a 400m field.

Panting, as we have seen, can be a natural response to certain activities without meaning anything serious. However, persistent panting for long periods may be a result of an underlying issue and may be worth visiting your Vernerian. Hence, always consider the other behaviors that accompany your dog's panting manner.

CHEWING

Not many dog owners recognize chewing as a means of communication in dogs. However, chewing is a behavior that can communicate different things when done together with other behaviors, some of which include the following:

- **Boredom.** Chewing in dogs could result from a lack of stimulation and insufficient mental or physical exercise, especially when accompanied by behaviors like pacing around, barking and excessively. In this case, such chewing is destructive as the dog would chew on anything it can get his teeth on.

- **Teething.** Puppies in the teething stage would exhibit behaviors such as swollen gums, drooling, and a strong urge to chew on objects. They do this to ease the discomfort that comes with the teething phase.
- **Attention-seeking.** Dogs can sometimes be attention seekers, and one of the ways they do this is through chewing. Other things they do to provoke a response are nudging their owners, barking, or pawing at them.
- **Curiosity.** Dogs are good at using their mouths to investigate, so chewing is one of those behaviors they exhibit when exploring. In this case, other behaviors to look out for are nudging objects, intense sniffing, licking or biting on items, and an overall show of interest in their surroundings.
- **Stress.** As we've seen, stress could cause your dog to display a variety of behaviors, one of which is chewing. Other stress behaviors accompanied by chewing include loss of appetite, irregular sleep patterns, and hiding.

EATING UNSUITABLE THINGS

When your dog begins to eat wrong things, and by unsuitable, I mean non-edible items they should normally not consume, below are some meanings attached to such behavior:

- **Play.** Sometimes, it doesn't have to be that serious. Your dog might simply be using his mouth to explore his surroundings. This behavior is particularly common in young pups who are still getting used to their environment.
- **Attention-seeking.** If your dog has tried several ways to get your attention to no avail, he'll try something else to provoke a response from you. And if chewing unsuitable objects is what he has to do to get your attention, that's exactly what he'll do.
- **Boredom/ Lack of Mental Stimulation.** We have sound knowledge of the causes and effects of boredom at this point in the book, as we've discussed extensively some of the behaviors associated with boredom. If you leave your dog indoors for very long periods, it's not uncommon for them to begin chewing unsuitable things. This clearly indicates that you need to explore mentally and physically stimulating activities for your dog.
- **Nutritional Deficiency.** Otherwise known as pica, the common signs of nutritional deficiency include eating non-edible items, which is often a sign of a lack of minerals or vitamins in their diet.
- **Anxiety.** We've seen how dogs behave in different ways when faced with stress and anxiety. Although chewing on appropriate objects is considered destructive behavior, it could serve as a coping mechanism for stressed and anxious dogs to find comfort in their surroundings.

Eating and chewing on non-edible objects is an undesirable behavior in dogs you want to pay attention to as soon as possible. Make sure to provide the right toys for your dog and enough mental and physical stimulation to address this challenge. You may also want to consider visiting your veterinarian to be sure there are no underlying issues causing such behavior.

STEALING

Stealing is yet another undesirable behavior a dog is likely to show when a few things are not appropriately considered. If your dog begins to demonstrate this behavior, it could be telling you one of the following things:

- **Lack of training.** Dogs who lack proper training or clear boundaries are likely to steal. If they have not been trained on objects to take and what not to take, they'll grow to develop the habit of taking anything that catches their interest.
- **Resource guarding.** Resource guarding is a trait in dogs that makes them search for valuable resources such as toys, food, and even attention. To them, taking and guarding these resources could be a means of asserting control or possession over what they think should be theirs. Resource guarding is a natural desire in dogs that can be managed effectively with appropriate training.
- **Attention-seeking.** Don't be surprised if you see some reasons popping more than others; it's merely a cue on certain areas that need more attention when handling dogs. Your dog may steal objects around the home just to get attention from you or any of the family members. Possible responses they're trying to provoke are chasing games and interaction.
- **Lack of stimulation.** A dog may result to stealing objects if that would give him the excitement he would otherwise get if he had been mentally and physically stimulated. If you're wondering about some of the exercises to provide adequate stimulation, we'll have more than enough as we gradually make progress to the next section of this book.

Stealing is never an appropriate behavior, especially not for our beloved pets. Ensure your dog has enough chew toys and a variety of activities to keep them engaged both mentally and physically.

However, if this behavior persists over time, then you should consider booking a meeting with a professional dog behaviorist for better guidance training.

WHINING

Whining is one of the many ways dogs communicate. Below are some of the possible reasons behind their whining.

- **Anxiety/Restlessness.** Your dog would whine if he's in an environment that's making him restless. Other body languages to look out for in this case are the dog's body posture, lowered head, raised hackles, and difficulty settling down.
- **Attention-seeking.** It's also common for dogs to whine, seeking excitement, interaction, or fun time. You also want to pay attention to their vocalization and intensity of vocalization, as these can provide additional insight into what they're trying to tell you.
- **Pain/Discomfort.** Dogs often communicate pain and discomfort through whining. Most times, it could be a sign that they're feeling sick or some kind of physical pain. Be sure to examine all parts of your dog's body, eye contact, and overall demeanor for additional cues.
- **Specific needs.** Dogs may whine if they need specific needs to be met, such as food, water, or want to go outside for a break.

Whining in dogs is usually accompanied by other body languages to help you better understand the reason for his whining. Hence, it is important to consider all of these, together with the context to better interpret his intentions.

DIGGING

Digging is a natural instinct in dogs that dates back to their early ancestry. However, digging in dogs may convey various messages, some of which include the following:

- **Need for mental and physical stimulation.** Your dog may begin to dig around to eliminate boredom and find something to do if they aren't getting enough mental and physical stimulation.
- **Denning or comfort.** Denning is an ancient behavior in the wolf family, indicating where they build for retreat and shelter. Dogs, as we know, are part of the generic wolf family. So, when you see your dog digging up on a hot day or chilling under the kitchen when it's raining cats and dogs, it's simply their denning instincts kicking in for shelter and comfort.
- **Hiding Treasure.** Some dogs find it fun to bury prized possessions such as favorite toys or a treat for safety. However, they tend to forget the exact place they buried these objects, which results in more digging in search of their hidden treasure.
- **Escape/Exploration.** If, for some reason, your dog wants to leave the house, digging under the fence sounds like a more sensible thing to do than trying to go over it. In most cases, this behavior is triggered by your dog's desire to get something at the other side of the fence- a toy or another dog.

BITING

As sweet and social dogs are, it's important to note that any dog can bite. Dogs don't bite for no reason (with exceptions to very rare cases); it is always a reaction to something. Dogs could vary from small nicks to serious bites that might require medical attention.

There are often warning signs- barking, snapping or growling- a dog gives before barking but is unfortunately misunderstood by people. Typically, a dog tries to communicate his discomfort at something or someone before biting. Let's look at some of the messages he's trying to convey.

- **Fear.** Most aggression from dogs comes from a place of fear and trying to protect themselves or their own. As the perceived threat gets closer, the dog becomes overwhelmed and may respond to such a reaction by barking. The dog is biting out of fear, basically trying to create a distance between himself and the threat.
- **Startle.** Dogs respond to startling by biting. It is not a good idea to startle a sleeping dog as this could cause them confusion, which may possibly lead to unplanned bites. These kinds of bites tend to take people even by surprise as they would ordinarily not react in such a way. It is vital to teach kids not to crawl up dogs-especially the older ones with possibly reduced hearing and visual strength- or wake them when they are asleep.
- **Pain.** Physical discomfort as a result of sickness or injury could be stressful and overwhelming for dogs. Even the friendliest of dogs tend to bite when in pain. Hence, you want to be cautious around your injured dog, especially in how you move him around.

- **Frustration.** Nobody likes to be trapped in an unpleasant situation or environment, not even dogs. If your dog perceives his environment to be unpleasant or annoying, he does what he can to leave such a scene. However, he feels frustrated when he's been held back, which may result in biting whatever (or whoever) is holding him back.
- **Protecting.** Dogs, just like humans, don't like their valuables taken away from them. In such cases, they respond to biting out of fear that their precious toy or food is being taken away from them. It's also common for dogs to have guard tendencies, which may result in them biting if they sense an intruder coming to their home or a member of their family is in danger, even though it might necessarily be real.

YOUR DOG NEEDS

As a dog owner, your ability to understand the needs and preferences of your dog plays a crucial part in your relationship with your dog. The better you understand these differences, the better the chances of your dog leading a fulfilling life with you.

In this section, we'll take a closer look at the various aspects of dog needs- breed characteristics, personalities, and age-related requirements.

BREED CHARACTERISTICS

Humans have been breeding dogs as far back as ancient times. Over the years, dogs have been bred for various reasons. As a result, today, we have dogs with varying temperaments, energy levels, and physical traits. Understanding dog breed characteristics is vital to help you effectively meet the needs of your dog. Below are the characteristics of dogs according to their breeds:

1. **Energy Levels**

Dog breeds with <u>high energy levels</u> include:
- Siberian Huskies
- Border Collies
- Kelpies
- Australian Shepherds
- Cattle Dogs

Under the right training conditions and environment, high-energy dogs do well as exercise companions and enthusiastic and interactive home buddies.

On the other hand, <u>low-energy dogs</u> are more inclined towards leisurely activities.
Common low-energy breeds include:
- Basset Hounds
- Bulldogs
- Bloodhound
- Bichon Frise
- Boston Terrier

Low energy doesn't translate to zero energy. They're an ideal choice for people who live in a small apartment and can do without having their pup jumping all over the furniture seeking various means to engage their high energy levels. Common low-energy breeds include:

1. **Temperaments**
   You've most likely seen dogs that are highly sociable, even with visitors and others that prefer to be reserved and on their own.

   Sociable dog breeds include the following:
   - Labrador Retriever
   - Golden Retriever
   - Beagle
   - Irish Settler
   - Bichon Frise
   - Cavalier King
   - Bernese Mountain

   On the other hand, dogs with more aloof personalities include:
   - Akita
   - Chow Chow
   - Afghan Hound
   - Siberian Husky
   - Saluki

   It's possible for dogs to have high energy levels yet be distant and reserved, as in the case of Siberian Huskies, Chow Chow, and Saluki. Though very friendly and fun to be with when around family, they are often wary and tend to be protective of their family when around strangers.

PERSONALITIES

Here, it is important to note that dog personalities are not determined by their breeds. It is possible to have the same breed with varying personalities. In this case, you want to pay close attention to your dog's personality when addressing certain matters. Important personality traits to consider include:

1. **Sensitivity.** Some dogs are more sensitive to physical and mental stimuli than others. For example, how sibling pups respond to noise, touch, and environmental cues may be different as it is perfectly normal. Hence, it is crucial to pay attention to the sensitivity of your dog(s) and provide a safe space for them to thieve based on their personality.
2. **Sociability.** Some dogs are extroverted by nature, while others are more reserved and prefer being in the company of family only. It doesn't mean something is wrong with them; it's just traits rooted in their personalities, as we have with humans. What you can do is create an environment where your dog can thrive in a manner that suits his personality.

AGE AND LIFE STAGES

As a dog owner, you must understand that your dog's needs will change as they grow into different life stages. So, as you train your dog, you want to consider taking care of them according to age requirements, as what appeals to a younger pup may not be the same with an older dog. Basically, the life stages of a dog can be divided into:

1. Puppyhood. Puppyhood refers to the early stages of a dog's life, starting from birth and progressing gradually until they reach Adolescence. The duration of puppyhood of a dog is dependent on its breed and individuality. However, the typical puppyhood stage can be anywhere from six to eighteen months. Notable milestones in puppyhood include the following:

- **Neonatal stage (0-2 weeks):** At this stage, the dog might not yet be able to see, hear or interact with his surroundings. He is fully dependent on his mother and spends most of his time sleeping and nursing.
- **Transitional stage (2-4 weeks):** Slowly but surely, their eyes begin to open, their other senses develop gradually, and they begin to move around with their siblings as they explore their new home.
- **Socialization Stage (3-14 weeks):** This is an essential period of puppyhood for socialization and learning. At this stage, puppies begin to develop social skills, learn a few things from their mother as well as siblings, and further explore their surroundings. It is crucial that you expose them to other dogs (or animals), people, and the environment, as these play an important role in their overall experience and interaction with people and their surroundings.
- **Juvenile stage (3-6 months):** Puppies gradually grow to be independent and start teething. They continue to learn more about their environment, and you'll begin to see significant changes in their energy levels. This is a good stage of puppyhood to introduce basic mental and physical training.

2. Adolescent age: This marks the end of puppyhood and the beginning of adulthood. They gradually reach sexual maturity and begin to exhibit signs like more independence, testing boundaries and increased bouts of energy. You also should be consistent in reinforcing behaviors such as:

- Obedience
- Mental stimulation
- Calmness and Impulse
- Health and Safety
- Grooming and Veterinary visits
- Good Manners
- Recall commands

In addition to training and teaching them these behaviors, use positive reinforcement techniques-treats, praise, and toys- to encourage desired behaviors you want in them.
Lastly, remember to be patient and consistent in training your dog as they are key elements of shaping your dog to mature into a desirable, fulfilling adult dog.

3. Adult Dogs. Dogs typically become adults from Adolescence till their seventh year. At this stage, their energy levels and personalities are established and evident in how they live. They thrive on regular exercise, which includes lots of mental and physical stimulation, a good diet, and routine veterinary care to ensure they don't suffer any health or age-related challenges.

4. Senior Dogs. This is the stage where dogs begin to experience changes in how they respond to physical and mental stimuli. And as such, you should be able to make certain adjustments in areas like nutrition, exercise routine, and medical care to cater to their changing needs. Other things that may change as they age into senior dogs include regular veterinary checkups and more comfortable resting space.

CONCLUSION

As a dog owner, understanding your dog is a fact that cannot be overemphasized, as you can tell from the volume of this chapter. It is your duty and responsibility to be able to understand your dog and identify his needs at various stages of his life.

Over the course of this chapter, we discussed the various ways to recognize different moods in dogs, canine communication, and understanding the need of dogs based on certain factors.

As you implement what you've learned so far, remember to treat each dog as an individual. This will play an important role in helping you understand and adapt to your dog(s) needs, which ultimately leads to better bonding and relationship between you and your dog.

In the next chapter, we will cover more interesting grounds in this book as we explore the essentials in getting us started with training our dogs to become desirable pets. For all of that and more, I'll see you in the next chapter.

CHAPTER 3
TRAINING ESSENTIALS FOR BEGINNERS

Having a dog as the newest member of the family is no doubt a pleasant experience. However, it involves a lot of work as we have seen in the previous chapter- from understanding his moods, emotions, body language and personality. With that out of the way, it's time to venture into one of the most important commitments any dog owner must make to their dog-building a good bond and communication through training.

Since we will be discussing the essentials in this chapter, you wouldn't be needing much to get started with training your furry friend, however, proper guidance will be needed. There are many ways to train a dog. It's easy to get lost in one of the several ways you'd find on TV, the internet, and even the bookstore.

However, not all of these methods have been tested, neither do the align with the science of learning. As a result, at the core of some of these trainings are practices accompanied with fear pain, and intimidation, which defeats the purpose of building a great bond for you and your dog.

On the other hand, effective, science-based training depends on identifying what motivates your dog to learn-food, outdoors, play- and using it as a way to positively reinforce those behaviors you want him to learn. If you realize your dog finds it difficult to make progress during training, there could be a few simple fixes. First, you want to find out the quality of the reward-if it is appealing to him or not- or the nature of the distraction.

Sometimes, the environment you're trying to train a dog in might not be so conducive for him. You may want to consider training him somewhere quieter and try to break down your goal into smaller steps for him. Remember, learning, just as it is with humans, doesn't follow a linear path. So, if your dog is not catching up for one reason or the other, consider giving him some space and time to catch up. He could be one of those dogs with a shy personality.

ESSENTIALS TO BEGIN

This section is essential for laying the right foundation for a successful training program with your dog. In this section, we will explore the basic steps in creating a daily training routine with your dog and following up with consistency. In addition, we emphasize the importance of setting boundaries, dedicated periods and areas for training, rules for carefree training to create an environment suitable for your dog, and the importance of engaging all family members in the training process.

There's a lot to discuss here; let's jump right in!

HOW MUCH TIME DO YOU NEED TO START A SIMPLE TRAINING ROUTINE?

The first step to embark on a training program for your dog is to create appropriate time every day for your dog's mental exercise. These creatures thrive best on routine; hence, it is vital to set aside time for training each day.

For example, you can have your morning and evening training sessions after breakfast and dinner respectively, both sessions lasting about 10 to 15 minutes of engaging and mentally stimulating exercises (for starters). By incorporating a consistent training routine with your dog, it arouses enthusiasm in him, making him look forward to the next training session after his breakfast and dinner. The more you do this, the more receptive he becomes to learning and training.

As you begin to notice higher energy levels and engagement in your dog, you may then begin to gradually increase the duration of his training sessions to match his energy level.

TIPS FOR ESTABLISHING AN EFFECTIVE TRAINING ROUTINE WITH YOUR DOG

Having established the importance of training routine, let's now take look at some steps to help us achieve this:

- **Be clear on training goals.** Your first step should be to determine what you want to achieve through the training. It could be anything from basic obedience commands, such as sit, stay, come, run off, to more advanced behaviors and tricks. Being clear on your goal is essential in guiding you through the training session.

- **Allocate time for training.** Go through your daily schedule and apportion time for training sessions with your dog. You don't need to spend long hours training them at a stretch. Anywhere from 10 to 15 minutes of mentally stimulation activities should be just fine for a training session. And like we mentioned earlier, it should be a time when you and your dog are focused and ready for training- in the morning or early hours of the evening.

- **Select appropriate training space.** Designate an environment in your house free of distractions as your dog's training space. This could be a specific area in the house or somewhere in the yard. Also, ensure to be consistent in whichever area you choose, and that the place is safe for the dog and large enough for him to move freely.

- **Start with the basics.** Obedience training sets the foundation of every other form of training. Hence, you want to reinforce basic commands such as sit and stay. Once they begin to respond to these commands, you may begin to introduce additional commands. In addition to starting with the basics, you also want to focus on one command per training session. You don't want to overwhelm your dog with too many commands at the same time.

- **Employ positive reinforcements.** We've mentioned quite a bit about the importance of positive reinforcement in training as a means of rewarding your dog for doing the right thing. Set aside tasty treats or favorite toys for your dog to reinforce desired behaviors. Whenever they make a correct response, you can also use a positive tone to praise them to reinforce such response in future.

- **Stay consistent.** Consistency is key when it comes to training dogs. Ensure you use the same commands, signals, and techniques throughout the training process. The more consistent you are with your training style. The easier your associate appropriate cues with a desired action. And it's not just you; teach every family member to be consistent with the same training techniques to avoid confusion between family members and the dog.

- **Progress gradually.** If you stay consistent in your training process, it's only a matter of time before your dog becomes very responsive and proficient with the basic commands. Once you notice this, you may gradually introduce more advanced training to expand their command repertoire. The key to gradual progression is building on the foundational commands already established to teach them new tricks, focus exercises, and impulse control.

- **Make the training fun.** All training and no fun would eventually tire your dog out. To avoid this, mix training activities with play to make it enjoyable for him. Reward your dog with a fun play session after every session. This could even serve as a means of positive reinforcement, which ultimately enhances the bond between you and your dog.

In summary, three elements are essential in training your dog, especially at the basic level. These are patience, consistency, and positive reinforcement. Ensure to continually reinforce older commands to refresh their memory. If you do these, you're well on the path of reaping the benefits of a well-trained and mentally stimulated dog.

EASY RULES FOR CAREFREE PLAYING

Playtime constitutes an essential part of a dog's mental exercise. However, you want to make sure that playtime is safe, fun, and engaging for you and your dog. Below are some easy rules to follow:

- **Teach your dog patience.** Teach your dog to remain calm and composed before initiating a play by using specific commands such as "Wait" or "Stay." This helps them put their excitement in check and wait for your approval before engaging.

- **Encourage gentle play.** Dogs could go over and beyond during playtime. Hence, ensure to discourage all rough behaviors by directing their attention to their favorite toys or other activities. This rule helps create boundaries for dogs to enjoy safe play as well as for others playing with them.

- **Set playtime boundaries.** It is your responsibility to determine areas where play is allowed, places off-limits, and objects that can be used during playtime. Establishing playtime boundaries tailor your dog's playtime to appropriate boundaries, discourages destructive behaviors, and helps your dog differentiate between household items and toys to prevent destructive chewing.

- **Keep an eye on them.** Ensure to supervise your dog, especially when they're getting used to a new toy or having fun with other dogs. This is vital for the safety of all dogs and also for you to interfere if any dog exhibits an undesirable behavior that could be harmful to himself or others.

Carefree playing is not about leaving your dog to play just anyhow. It is about creating an environment where they exercise mentally and physically and have an overall enjoyable experience.

THE IMPORTANCE OF INVOLVING ALL FAMILY MEMBERS IN TRAINING

Involving all family members in the training process is essential in the training process if you want to achieve the best results. Below are some of the reasons why you want all members of the family involved:

- **Consistency in training techniques and commands.** Apart from routine, dogs tend to do better when communication is clear. Involving all family members in the training process reduces the possibility of confusion, allows the dog to understand the command regardless of who gives it, and for an overall harmonious training experience.

- **Improves the bond between the dog and the family.** Dog training goes beyond giving dogs commands and helping them respond appropriately. It is also an opportunity for the dong to bond with every family member. When all family members are actively involved in the dog's training and development, it deepens the intimacy between the dog and the family.

- **Shared responsibility.** The duty of training a dog in the family should not be exclusively for one person. If anything, it takes quite a lot to train a dog from puppyhood to become a desired household furry member of the family. Involving all family members in the training process shares the responsibility, making it more manageable and sustainable in the long run. This way, family members get to share tips and different training perspectives, which could be beneficial for the progress of the dog's training.

This inclusive training process allows for a supportive environment that enables the dog to generalize his training with every member of the family unit as well as his environment.

COMMON MISTAKES TO AVOID WHEN TRAINING YOUR DOG

As you venture into the journey of training your dog, it is vital to be aware of common mistakes that may get in the way of your progress and consequently affect the effectiveness of your training efforts. Understanding these mistakes helps create a fulfilling training experience for you and your dog.

- **Punishment-based training.** One of the quickest ways to defeat the whole purpose of training your dog is by relying on punishment as a method of training. Punishing your dog-verbally or physically-creates fear and anxiety in your dog. And if you followed the book carefully to this point, you know that no good could come out of these two emotions.
Rather than using punishment as a tool, a better alternative we've seen is using positive reinforcement, rewarding desired behaviors, and redirecting unwanted behaviors to something they're already familiar or engaged with.

- **Inconsistent training:** Inconsistency in anything-rules, commands or signals could lead to confusion and slow down the learning process. Ensure that all family members adopt the same training techniques and consistently reinforce boundaries to eliminate room for confusion.

- **Ignoring mental stimulation.** The importance of mental stimulation in dogs is a significant part of this book that we will be addressing in the next session. It is such a big deal because failure to do this opens the door to feelings of restlessness, boredom, or destructive behavior in dogs. Activities such as scent games, puzzle toys, and many more (that we will cover in great detail) help challenge your dog's mind and keep them positively engaged. This way, they're less likely to engage in undesirable behaviors.

- **Lack of patience.** Good things take time, and you'll agree with me that training your dog is a good thing. As a dog owner, you must be patient to allow your dog(s) to learn at their respective places. Don't try to rush the training process or expect instant results. Instead, practice patience, and give them the right guidance and positive reinforcement to keep them going. Remember, training is a gradual process, and every action responded well to is a cause to celebrate.

ABOUT TOYS

Games play a fundamental role in stimulating our four-legged friends. Just like with children, our dogs also get excited when they receive something new. Games stimulate their curiosity, ignite emotions, and help us teach them new things.
However, as quickly as we can capture their attention, we often see them getting bored with the same games. That's why it's important to keep their curiosity alive through interactive play and dedicate time and attention to it. Above all else, our dogs need care and attention. That's why no matter how technological or expensive a game may be, it can never replace quality time spent together, a walk, or a cuddle session.

Too often, dogs are left alone for long hours at home because our work schedules don't allow otherwise. If this is also the case for you, always remember that you don't need to buy games that they will quickly grow tired of. Simply try to bring more quality into the hours you have available. Explore some of the games you can find in this book. Just 10-15 minutes of attentive play and stimulation can improve your bond and lead to highly satisfying results.

WHAT TO BUY AND HOW

While toys are good, being able to select the ones that cater to your dog's size, age, and chewing habits is equally important. A smaller toy, for instance, would appeal better to a pup than an adult dog. On the other hand, a larger toy would be more fitting for larger breeds.
When buying toys, it is important to consider interactive toys- puzzle toys or treat dispensing toys- as they are more engaging, prevent boredom, and make your dog more mentally alert.

In addition, you should also carefully select toys made of materials that can withstand your dog's energy level and chewing habits.

SURPRISE YOUR DOG WITH DIY TOYS

Not all toys are bought from the store. You could create DIY toys in a few steps that perform the assignment just as well as the ones we purchase at the store.
DIY toys are cost-effective and allow you to explore your creativity to provide your dog with mental and physical activities during its playtime.

In the section dedicated to exercises and games, you will find several ideas for creating games with recycled materials that you already have at home. You have probably already noticed that our pets are very attracted to common materials, those objects we use in our daily lives, such as boxes, packaging, shoes, small toys belonging to your children or grandchildren…

Starting from these things, with a little creativity, you can build a large number of interesting games at no cost to stimulate their intelligence, propose new activities that won't bore them, and introduce interesting variations that gradually increase the level of strategy required to obtain a reward.

You will realize how much fun this will be for him and also for you.

In the book, you will find many DIY proposals. In each of these games and exercises, you will see the DIY category mentioned before the description.

Just one last thing before we begin: Do you remember what we talked about regarding the importance of easy rules for carefree playing? It is important that you supervise your dog while playing with these DIY toys primarily for their safety and to prevent cases of accidental ingestion of small parts of the toys.

CONCLUSION

The goal of this chapter is to get you up and running with the basics of training and interacting with your dog mentally and physically. It is important that we have a good understanding and are all on the same page regarding the topics we discussed in this chapter to provide a better transition from this theoretical section to a more practical section, where we will explore in great depth some of the best mental exercises for dogs from basic to advanced. For all of that and more, I will see you in the next session.

PART 2 - EXERCISES SECTION

After a long yet informative theoretical segment, I'd like to welcome you to the second section of this book, where we go in-depth into mental exercises for dogs. In this part, we'll do less explaining and see more examples and illustrations to make it as simple as possible for all readers to grasp the concept.

This section aims to provide you with a plethora of mentally-stimulating exercises to choose from. Each example has been carefully selected and categorized based on its difficulty level and other factors we will look into shortly.

Just before we go into the meat and potatoes of the section, if you have little or no idea where to start, I recommend you begin at the Basic level. I would like you to treat this section similarly to how you would if you just started working out in the gym. You don't get a ripped body after working out on your first day there. It takes patience and consistency to achieve worthwhile results. Furthermore, as you read, you'll realize that you don't have to exhaust all the exercises in this book to reap its full benefits. However, what's important is that you start somewhere, create a routine, and stick to it.

Note that each exercise has been carefully selected to cater to the different stages of a dog's life (as we've discussed in the previous section). This implies that there is always an exercise for every stage (birth to adulthood) of your pet's life.

With time and consistency, each exercise will become easier for your dog. The easier it becomes, the less stimulating it gets over time. Hence, the need for progressive overload and switching things up to continually stimulate your dog during every training session.

STRUCTURE:

All exercises described in this section will follow the same framework (as we'll see below) for consistency and to ensure we're all on the same page regardless of our experience in handling dogs before picking up this book.

After much consideration, I decided to adopt the following pattern for each exercise:

1. Name

2. Category: This refers to the classification or grouping of the exercise based on its nature of focus. In the context of this book- mental exercise for Dogs- various categories include the following:

- Kids games
- Food games
- Agility games
- Hunting and prey-related games
- DIY games
- Focus games
- Balancing games
- Impulse control games
- Water and diving games
- Search and scent games
- Intelligence and brain games (IQ games)
- Left alone games
- Indoor games
- Outdoor games

Categorizing the exercises in this manner helps to organize and understand the different activities that provide mental stimulation for dogs.

3. Objective: This describes the specific goals or targets that the exercise aims to achieve. Some of our objectives for these activities include:

- Improved problem-solving skills
- Enhanced mental agility
- Improved focus and impulse control
- Strengthening dog-owner bond

And the overall mental well-being of the dog.

4. Description: This helps the reader understand the mechanics and process of each exercise, step-by-step instructions, and any specific guidelines to perform the exercise correctly and effectively.

5. How to Play/Perform: This section of each exercise provides a systematic guide on how to carry out the exercise. It includes detailed instructions, steps, and techniques to follow in order to engage in the activity correctly. This includes information on setting up the exercise area, introducing cues or commands, demonstrating appropriate body language, and providing necessary precautions.

6. Important Tips

7. Recommended Repetitions: This refers to the suggested number of times an exercise should be repeated to achieve desirable results. This may vary depending on factors such as your dog's age, attention span, energy level, and individual progress. It is important to strike a balance between providing enough repetition for positive reinforcement and practicing without wearing your dog out.

With the introduction and structure of the section out of the way, let's now proceed to cover more interesting grounds. For all of that and more, I'll see you in the next chapter and the first exercise.

MENTAL EXERCISE
BASIC LEVEL

I use the term "Basic" to describe this category because it is meant to be simple with little to no complications at all. This basic level of mentally-stimulating exercises provides the base (or starting point) upon which other levels of difficulty can be built.

As we've stated earlier in the introduction, the basic level, as well as other levels that follow subsequently, will have similar subdivisions, with their difference being in the intensity of the games and probably the duration.

SNIFF AND SEEK

Category: Search and scent games

Objectives

The goal of Sniff and Seek is to encourage dogs to use their sense of smell to locate hidden objects or treats. This exercise helps them tap into their natural instincts, improves their olfactory skills, and enhances their overall mental stimulation. Sniff and Seek also provides an avenue for both you and your dog to have an enjoyable experience while working to improve his cognitive abilities.

Description

Sniff and Seek is a mentally-stimulating game that requires dogs to tap into their natural scenting abilities. Dogs have a great sense of smell, and this game helps them maximize this ability by encouraging them to smell treats or hidden objects around them.

How To Perform

1. **Start by choosing a suitable location:** Note that this game can be played indoors and outdoors. Wherever you choose, ensure the environment is free from distractions and potential hazards.
2. **Gather your dog's desirable treats or toys:** You want to have small bits of appealing treats or toys that your dogs can easily detect using their sense of smell.
3. **Hide the items:** Try to hide these treats in designated areas while your dog observes you. For starters, make the hiding spots easier to find, and as soon as your dog becomes more experienced, you may start hiding in more difficult-to-find areas.
4. **Give your dog a cue:** Cues such as "Find It!" or "Search!" are some of the most common ones used to tell a dog that it's time to search for a hidden item. However, ensure you are consistent with whatever cue you choose so that your dog can associate such cues with the game.
5. **Let your dog use his nose:** Observe your dog as he goes on the hunt. Also, encourage him to use his nose to explore the areas around him and track down objects.
6. **Provide positive reinforcement:** Once your dog successfully finds a hidden item, reward him with praise, physical affection, or enthusiastic encouragement. You may also reward him with a special treat specifically reserved for the game to make it more exciting in the end.
7. **Gradually make it more challenging:** It's only a matter of time before your dog becomes more proficient in this game. Once you notice this, gradually increase the difficulty of the hiding spots to make it more challenging, and continually help improve his scenting abilities.

Recommended Repetitions

The number of repetitions for this game depends on factors such as your dog's age and fitness level. Basically, start with shorter sessions of about 5 to 10 minutes and gradually increase the duration as your dog becomes more proficient. Also, aim to strike a balance to mke the game a challenging yet enjoyable one.

CANINE CASTLE

Category: Indoor games

Objectives

The objective of the Canine Castle is to create a dynamic and stimulating indoor challenge using household items. This exercise, coupled with its dynamic nature, improves mental engagement, physical coordination, and problem-solving in dogs, allowing for a stronger bond between dogs and their owners.

Description

Canine Castle is an interactive and mentally-stimulating indoor activity for dogs that tests their problem-solving abilities, agility, and creativity. It involves setting up little obstacles using household items to challenge your dog's mental and physical abilities.

How To Perform

1. **Choose a designated area:** Select somewhere spacious in the house to set up the canine castle.
2. **Gather tools for the castle:** Items used for the castle could be anything from blankets, hula hoops, boxes, small stools, or any other stable object that is least likely to cause harm while playing the game.
3. **Design the castle:** Do so in a manner that creates a series of challenges for your dog. There are no textbook means to design a castle in this case. You could do anything from building tunnels made from blankets or cardboard boxes, climbing over low stools, and weaving through hula hoops.
4. **Introduce your dog to the castle:** Allow your dog to take a look at the Canine Castle without him engaging it at first. Let him sniff around to find the obstacles at his own pace.
5. **Interact with him:** Don't leave your dog alone to do all the heavy lifting. Provide him with some verbal cues and gestures throughout the course of the game and encourage him with positive reinforcement when he successfully completes a challenge.
6. **Increase difficulty:** As your dog becomes more comfortable deciphering the castle, you can gradually increase the difficulty level by adding new obstacles to the castle or rearranging the existing ones. This helps keep the game continually challenging yet engaging as it improves your dog's problem-solving capabilities.

Recommended Repetitions

The amount of repetition of the Canine Castle can vary based on your dog's focus and energy level. As usual, start the game with shorter sessions (around 10 to 15 minutes), and increase the duration as your dog starts to get the hang of it.

You may practice Canine Castle with your dog a few times a week to keep his body and mind sound. Ensure that all items used for the castle are stable and safe.

TOY TREASURE HUNT

Category: Indoor games, Search and scent games

Objectives

Toy Treasure Hunt is designed to tap into your dog's innate instincts and provide a mentally stimulating and rewarding experience. This exercise promotes mental agility, improves focus, and deepens the connection between you and your dog by engaging his senses, natural hunting skills, and problem-solving abilities.

Description

Transform your home into a captivating adventure land for your dog with the Toy Treasure Hunt game. This mentally-stimulating exercise perfectly blends the thrill of hide-and-seek and the excitement of discovering their favorite toys.

How To Perform

1. **Select a designated search area:** Select a location in your house spacious enough to accommodate this exercise. It could be your backyard, living room, etc., however, ensure the area is safe and free from any potential hazards.
2. **Gather the treasures:** Collect a variety of toys your dog finds interesting. Ensure the toys are in good condition and safe to play with.
3. **Hide the treasures:** Hide the toys in different areas within the search area. Start with easier hiding spots such as under cushions or behind furniture. As your dog becomes more experienced in the hunt, you may gradually increase the difficulty level of the search location.
4. **Provide cues for your dog:** Cues are good for arousing enthusiasm in dogs. Introduce commands such as "Go, (your dog's name)" or "Find your toys" to signal to him that it's time for him to hunt for his "treasures". Remember to remain consistent in your cues and commands.
5. **Unleash the hunter:** Release your dog and encourage him to explore the search area using his senses. Don't forget to provide verbal encouragement and praise all through the search process.
6. **Offer positive reinforcement:** When your dog successfully finds a hidden toy, celebrate his success by praising him enthusiastically, providing a special treat, or offering him physical affection as a means to reinforce his accomplishment and make it a joyful experience for him.
7. **Switch things up:** Varying the hiding spots is essential to keep the game engaging each time you play. Explore different areas in the house to hide toys. You could also make it more interesting by placing the toys at heights above the floor, under overturned baskets, or inside boxes.

Recommended Repetitions

Your dog's energy level and attention span are two factors that determine how often you can repeat this exercise. 10 to 15 minutes is okay for a start, then increase gradually as you notice your dog's interest and excitement increase.
Coupled with other exercises, playing this game 3 to 4 times per week is enough to provide adequate stimulation and entertainment for your dog.

TICK TRAINING EXTRAVAGANZA

Category: Kids games

Objectives

Tick Training Extravaganza aims to improve your dog's focus, agility, and obedience through tick training. This exercise promotes impulse control and grooms the ability of your dog to respond appropriately to your cues by associating specific "ticks" with commands and rewarding correct responses. Tick training is also important to strengthen the bond between the dog and other family members by developing impulse control and responsiveness to the commands of family members.

Description

Tick Training is a game designed to boost interactivity while teaching obedience and stimulating your dog's cognitive circuitry. This exercise involves the use of "tick training", where your dog learns to respond to gentle touches or "ticks".

How To Perform

1. **Select a suitable stage:** You want an area free of distractions where you can conduct this exercise. A spacious room, backyard, or anywhere safe and secure is fine.
2. **Give the tick signal:** Choose a specific touch or tick motion—a light stroke or a gentle tap on his shoulder—to serve as a unique prompt for your dog. Note that this touch should be one that would be easy for your dog to distinguish from other physical contact.
3. **Provide a reward:** The exercise is not complete without a good reward for your dog. His reward could be anything from tasty treats to favorite toys or anything he finds interesting and motivating.
4. **Start by introducing basic commands:** It is essential that you inculcate basic commands such as "Sit," "Stay," or "Down." Once you give the command verbally, follow it with its corresponding signal. For example, when you say "Sit," you immediately gently tap the shoulder.
5. **Reinforce correct commands:** You are to provide immediate positive reinforcement as soon as your dog gets a command correctly.
6. **Progress to more advanced commands:** As soon as your dog becomes familiar with the basic commands, you may begin to gradually introduce more advanced ones such as "Fetch," "Shake hands," or "Roll over." Using the same technique, give the verbal command, accompanied by the corresponding tick signal, and reward the correct response.
7. **Introduce controlled distractions:** Incorporating distractions makes the game more challenging for your dog. However, it helps train his impulse control and ability to focus. Distractions such as having someone walk by, making gentle noise, or dropping a toy nearby should do the trick. Continue with the command and tick even with these distractions; they are great for helping dogs maintain their focus.

Recommended Repetitions

The number of times you repeat this training is dependent on your dog's individual progress and learning capabilities. However, for starters, you should aim to practice this exercise a few times per week with shorter training sessions of about 5 to 10 minutes. Starting small helps the dog to get proficient in the exercise, and practicing it a few times a week helps reinforce the training and maintain your dog's responsiveness.

PUPPY PARTY GAMES

Category: Outdoor games, Indoor games, Kids games

Objectives

Puppy Party Games seek to provide a playful and interactive environment where puppies can harness essential skills while having fun with other pups. This game aims to enhance coordination, promote socialization, and develop a positive association with learning and play.

Description

As the name implies, the Puppy Party Games is a delightful activity designed to entertain and educate young pups in a social and playful setting. This game provides an avenue for pups to have fun while learning valuable skills. Games such as tug-of-war, puzzle challenges, obstacle challenges, etc., offer great mental and physical stimulation for pups.

How To Perform

1. **Set the play area:** Ensure the stage is safe and spacious enough to accommodate the pups. A large indoor space or backyard is a good option to get the ball rolling.
2. **Set up game stations:** Create various game stations such as "tug-of-war zone," "puppy puzzle challenge," and "ball pit bonanza" to keep the pups entertained.
3. **Tug-of-War Zone:** Set up a designated area where puppies can use dog-safe toys in a fair and friendly tug-of-war competition.
4. **Puppy Puzzle Challenge:** Provide your dogs with a variety of interactive puzzle toys that require them to stimulate their cognitive abilities and problem-solving skills to retrieve toys or treats.
5. **Ball Pit Bonanza:** Create a designated area of something similar to an inflatable pool and fill it with soft balls. Let the puppies dive in and explore. This game enhances their sensory stimulation and promotes coordination and social interaction.
6. **Encourage socialization:** Allow your pups to interact and play with each other under close supervision. Ensure that all puppies are comfortable and no form of bullying is allowed.
7. **Offer positive reinforcement:** Provide rewards by offering bits of delicious treats to your pups for their participation and good behavior during the games.

Recommended Repetitions

How long you play the Puppy Party Games depends on the puppies' age, energy level, and attention span. Shorter sessions of 15 to 20 minutes are encouraged to allow the puppies to rest and recharge between sessions.

These series of games can be quite overwhelming, hence, it is important that you take things one at a time. In addition to this, remember to repeat and switch the activities to reinforce their socialization skills and provide continual mental and physical stimulation.

TREAT TOWEL PUZZLE

Category: Search and scent games, DIY games

Objectives

The Treat Towel Puzzle exercise is designed to engage your dog's problem-solving abilities and provide mental stimulation in a small space. By creating a fun and interactive game with towels and treats, your dog will enjoy the challenge of unraveling the puzzle to uncover hidden rewards. This exercise promotes focus and patience and encourages your dog to use his cognitive skills while having a great time.

Description

The Treat Towel Puzzle exercise involves using two towels and a variety of tasty treats to create an engaging and rewarding game that will keep your dog entertained and mentally stimulated.

How To Perform

1. **Set up the puzzle:** Gather two towels, one small and one large. Place some treats in the small towel and tightly wrap them into a knot to create a treat bundle. Scatter additional treats on the large towel, as well as the small towel bundle, and fold the large towel into a knot or pretzel shape (with the small towel bundle wrapped inside it).
2. **Introduce the puzzle:** Hand your dog the large towel puzzle and use encouraging words, such as "Find the treats!" or "Solve the puzzle!" Use an excited and enthusiastic tone to engage your dog's interest and curiosity.
3. **Problem-solving challenge:** Encourage your dog to use his nose, paws, and mouth to manipulate the towel puzzle and uncover the hidden treats. Avoid giving direct instructions, and allow your dog to explore and figure out the puzzle on his own.
4. **Provide assistance:** Closely supervise your dog during the puzzle-solving process to prevent frustration or destructive behavior. If your dog gets stuck or seems frustrated, provide gentle guidance by pointing to the towel or giving verbal cues to keep him engaged.
5. **Reward and reinforce:** When your dog successfully retrieves treats from the puzzle, offer immediate praise and rewards. Use positive reinforcement, such as verbal cues like "Good job!" or additional treats, to reinforce his problem-solving efforts.
6. **Adjust the challenge:** Increase the difficulty of the puzzle over time by making the knots tighter or adding more layers to the towel. Introduce different textures or obstacles to further challenge your dog's problem-solving skills.

Important Tips:

- Use small, dog-friendly treats that easily fit within the towels.
- Always supervise your dog during the puzzle-solving activity to ensure their safety.
- Monitor the towels closely to prevent your dog from ingesting any threads or chewing the towels.
- Provide assistance and guidance when necessary to keep the game enjoyable and frustration-free.

Recommended Repetitions

Play the Treat Towel Puzzle game for approximately 10 to 15 minutes per session. This game can be played every day by adjusting the duration based on your dog's energy level and attention span.

PUZZLE FEEDER FRENZY

Category: Food games, DIY games

Objectives

The goal of the Puzzle Feeder Frenzy is to provide mental stimulation and enhance his problem-solving skills while making mealtime an enjoyable experience. Other objectives of this exercise include using problem-solving skills to access his food, preventing rapid eating, extending the duration of mealtime, and overall mental engagement and satisfaction.

Description

Puzzle Feeder Frenzy is an interactive food game that involves using specially-designed feeders or interactive toys to engage your dog's problem-solving instincts in working for his food. The process of figuring out his meals during this exercise makes it an enriching experience for dogs.

How To Perform

1. **Choose a puzzle feeder:** Select a puzzle feeder or interactive toy-puzzle bowls, dispensing balls, or maze-like toys, suitable for your dog's size, breed, and skill level.
2. **Introduce the puzzle feeder:** Get your dog familiarized with the puzzle feeder by letting him sniff around. Show him how it works by demonstrating how to interact with or manipulate the toy to access the food inside.
3. **Fill the puzzle feeder:** Place a portion of your dog's treat into the puzzle feeder. Ensure to adjust the difficulty level based on your dog's experience level. Start with easier puzzles and gradually progress into more advanced challenges.
4. **Present the puzzle feeder:** Present your dog with the puzzle feeder and encourage him with verbal cues such as "Get your food!" or "Find it!"
5. **Offer guidance when needed:** If your dog struggles to figure out the challenge, you may provide assistance on how to manipulate the puzzle. While you don't want to ruin the challenge by giving him direct answers, you can still provide the necessary guidance by nudging him in the right direction.
6. **Monitor the difficulty level:** Observe how your dog is doing and adjust the difficulty level of the feeder accordingly. Similarly, increase the difficulty level once your dog begins to understand the game.
7. **Reward and celebrate:** Reward your dog with praise, additional treats, or affection when he successfully retrieves the food from the puzzle feeder. Positive reinforcement helps him enjoy the process even though it may seem challenging.

Note

Puzzle Feeder Frenzy can also be a DIY activity! Below is a suggestion for creating a homemade puzzle feeder using materials you may already have at home.

Materials

- An empty plastic bottle (such as a water bottle or soda bottle)
- Scissors or a craft knife
- Dog treats or kibble

Instructions

- Start by removing any labels or stickers from the plastic bottle.
- Utilize either the scissors or a craft knife to create multiple small openings on the sides of the bottle. The quantity and dimensions of these holes may vary based on your dog's abilities and the size of the treats you intend to use. Ensure that the openings are sufficiently large to accommodate the treats.
- Load the bottle with your canine companion's preferred treats or dry food.
- Screw the cap back on tightly to secure the treats inside the bottle.
- Place the bottle on the floor or in your dog's play area.

How to Play

1. Introduce the puzzle feeder to your dog by placing it in front of him.
2. Encourage your dog to interact with the bottle and figure out how to access the treats inside.
3. As your dog explores and manipulates the bottle, the treats will start to fall out through the holes, providing a reward for his efforts.
4. You can make the game more challenging by adjusting the size and number of holes or by adding additional obstacles or layers to the puzzle feeder.

Important Tips

- Make sure the bottle is clean and free of any sharp edges or small pieces that could pose a choking hazard.
- Supervise your dog while playing with the puzzle feeder to ensure he is engaging with it safely and not attempting to chew or ingest the bottle.

Recommended Repetitions

Puzzle Feeder Frenzy can be incorporated into your dog's daily feeding routine. You could start with one or two feeding sessions per day, then gradually increase the frequency if desired. In addition, adjust the amount of food used in the puzzle feeder to ensure your dog gets his adequate dietary requirements. Also, look out for your dog's eating habits and adjust the repetitions based on their enjoyment and engagement with the exercise.

BUBBLE! BUBBLE!! BUBBLE!!!

Category: Kids games, DIY games

Objectives

The objective of Bubble Games is to encourage your dog's physical activity and mental engagement. The exercise aims to stimulate his senses, promote coordination and agility, and enhance his focus and tracking abilities. It also creates a positive association with physical exercise and outdoor play.

Description

Bubble Games is a delightful and interactive exercise that combines fun and physical activity for both dogs and kids. This exercise involves creating and playing with bubbles, which can be an exciting experience for your dog. The floating bubbles capture his attention, encourage movement, and provide mental stimulation. It's a playful way to engage with your dog and promote exercise while enjoying quality time together.

How To Perform

1. **Gather bubble solution and a bubble wand:** Prepare a safe and non-toxic bubble solution suitable for dogs. Use a bubble wand or any other tool designed for creating bubbles.
2. **Find an appropriate outdoor area:** Choose an open outdoor space, such as a backyard or a park, where your dog can freely move around without any obstructions.
3. **Introduce the bubbles:** Show your dog the bubble wand and let him sniff it to become familiar with the object. This will help build positive associations before the bubble play begins.
4. **Create bubbles:** Dip the bubble wand into the bubble solution, allowing it to absorb an adequate amount. Gently blow through the wand to create floating bubbles in the air.
5. **Encourage your dog to chase and pop the bubbles:** Guide your dog's attention towards the floating bubbles. You can point at them or use an excited tone of voice to capture his interest. Encourage him to chase, jump, and pop the bubbles with his paws or nose.
6. **Celebrate his success:** When your dog successfully pops a bubble, offer praise, treats, or enthusiastic verbal cues to reinforce his engagement and effort. Make it a positive and rewarding experience for them.
7. **Vary the bubble patterns and movements:** Create different bubble patterns, sizes, and movements to keep the game interesting and engaging for your dog. You can blow bubbles in a zigzag pattern, create a bubble tunnel for him to run through, or release clusters of bubbles for him to chase.
8. **Ensure supervision and safety:** Always supervise your dog during Bubble Games. Make sure he is in a safe environment, away from any hazards or distractions. Monitor his excitement levels and provide breaks if needed to prevent overexertion.

Note

While Bubble Games can be enjoyed by dogs of all ages and sizes, ensure that the bubble solution used is safe for your dog and doesn't cause any adverse reactions. Consult with your veterinarian if you have any concerns or questions about using bubble solutions specifically formulated for dogs.

Recommended Repetitions

The frequency and duration of Bubble Games can vary based on your dog's age, fitness level, and the weather conditions. Start with shorter play sessions of about 10 to 15 minutes and gradually increase the duration as your dog becomes more comfortable and engaged. Aim for regular playtime, incorporating Bubble Games into your dog's exercise routine a few times per week or as desired.

FEATHER FRENZY

Category: Hunting and prey-related games, DIY games

Objectives

The Feather Frenzy exercise is designed to make a dog connect with his natural hunting and chasing instincts. The objectives of this exercise include improving focus and concentration, stimulating the dog's senses, and satisfying his natural prey desire.

Description

Feather Frenzy is an interactive game that simulates the thrill of chasing and catching prey. It involves using a feathered toy or object that mimics the movement of a small animal—particularly a bird. This exercise engages the dog's senses of scent, sight, and sound, encouraging him to exhibit his natural hunting behaviors.

How To Perform

1. **Select a feathered toy:** Choose a specific feathered toy for this game. It should be light, easy to maneuver, and able to imitate the movement of prey. You can also consider building one at home using recycled materials, drawing inspiration from those available on the market. This game, in fact, triggers our dog's predatory instinct and usually breaks quickly. That's why I have learned to build them using ribbons and other objects that I already have at home.
2. **Choose a designated play area:** Ensure the area is free from obstacles that may harm the dog or hinder his movement.
3. **Get your dog's attention:** Capture your dog's attention by showing him the feathered toy and allowing him to see, hear, and sniff it. Make sure he is excited and ready to engage in the game.
4. **Start the movement:** Begin moving the feathered toy in a manner that imitates the fluttering movement of a bird or small animal. Use quick, short movements to create an unpredictable yet exciting pattern.
5. **Encourage chasing and catching:** Entice your dog to chase the feathered toy by moving it just out of his reach. Make it a bit of a challenge for him to catch it, but not too difficult. Allow him to pounce, jump, and make quick turns as he tries to capture the "prey."
6. **Reward successful catches:** Offer praise, rewards, or small treats when your dog successfully catches a feathered toy. This will help reinforce the behavior and associate the game with a positive experience.
7. **Switch things up:** Vary the speed, direction, and height of the feathered toy's movement to keep the game interesting and unpredictable. You could also mimic the behavior of different types of prey to keep him actively engaged.
8. **Establish boundaries:** Set clear boundaries for the game to ensure your dog does not go over and beyond. Ensure to teach him a cue or command to signal the start and end of the game.
9. **Practice control and impulse control:** Introduce moments of control and impulse control during the game by using commands such as "Wait" or "Leave it" to teach him to control his impulses and engage with the toy when given permission.

Recommended Repetitions

The repetition frequency for Feather Frenzy varies depending on your dog's energy level and focus. Start with shorter sessions and increase the duration as the dog becomes more comfortable. Aim for 5 to 10 minutes of playtime per session, with 2 to 3 sessions per week.

EYE CONTACT MASTERY

Category: Focus games

Objectives

The Eye Contact Mastery exercise aims to strengthen dog-owner relationships, improve dog focus and attention, and promote effective communication. Other goals associated with this exercise include teaching the dog to maintain eye contact on command, enhancing responsiveness to cues, and reinforcing his ability to focus even in distracting environments.

Description

Eye Contact Mastery is a game that encourages the dog to maintain eye contact with his owner. The exercise establishes a foundation of trust, respect, and communication between both parties, improving the dog's focus and attention skills and leading to better obedience and cooperation in other training situations.

How To Perform

1. **Choose a quiet environment:** A calm environment that is free of distractions will help your dog focus on the exercise without being distracted.
2. **Get your dog's attention:** Capture your dog's focus by holding his favorite treat or toy near your face. Make sure he's looking directly at you.
3. **Issue the command:** Use clear verbal commands such as "Look" or "Watch" to signal to your dog to maintain eye contact. Be consistent in the commands you use and ensure you say them in a friendly manner.
4. **Reward eye contact:** Give your dog an immediate reward when he makes eye contact with you. This could be treats, a favorite toy, or praising him. Also ensure the reward is one your dog finds interesting and exciting.
5. **Extend the duration:** Gradually increase the duration of the exercise before offering a reward. Start with a few seconds of maintaining eye contact and work up to longer periods.
6. **Gradually introduce distractions:** Once your dog gets the hang of it in a quiet environment, start practicing in different environments to increase the difficulty level. Introducing distractions helps the dog generalize the concept and maintain focus even in challenging situations.
7. **Introduce hand signals:** Incorporating hand signals along with verbal commands helps reinforce eye contact behavior. For example, pointing to your eyes while giving the "look" command would be helpful in the exercise.
8. **Use intermittent rewards:** As your dog becomes good at maintaining eye contact, eliminate immediate rewards and intermittent rewards—i.e., rewarding him at intervals or alternately. This helps reinforce the behavior while keeping him engaged.
9. **Expand training to real-life situations:** As your dog becomes proficient in training, start practicing Eye Contact Mastery in everyday activities such as walks, meals, and interactions with other people or animals. Continually reinforcing the behavior ensures it becomes second nature to your dog.

Recommended Repetitions

The number of repetitions for Eye Contact Mastery depends on your dog's learning pace and concentration level. Start with short sessions of 5 to 10 minutes, with multiple repetitions within each session. Practice this exercise at least 3 to 5 sessions a week with your dog to reinforce the desired behavior and maintain consistency.

NAME RECOGNITION RALLY

Category: Puppy games

Objectives

The objectives of this exercise are to strengthen the dog's name recognition, improve their focus and attention, and enhance responsiveness to their names even in distracting environments.

Description

Name Recognition Rally is a fun game that helps dogs respond to their names quickly and reliably. Over time, the dog establishes an association between his name and paying attention when called, which promotes effective communication and better control in various situations.

How To Perform

1. **Choose a quiet and comfortable environment:** Start in an environment where your dog feels comfortable, with minimal distractions. This environment plays an important role in helping the dog maintain focus.
2. **Start at close range:** Stand a few feet from your dog and call his name in a clear and upbeat tone. Make sure you've got his attention moving to the next step.
3. **Reward immediate response:** When you call his name, and he looks at you or acknowledges his name, praise or offer him a reward. Note that the reward should be provided immediately after the dog's correct response to reinforce the desired behavior.
4. **Increase the distance:** Gradually increase the distance between you and your dog as he becomes more proficient in responding to his name. Doing this helps him generalize this behavior and respond to his name even from a distance.
5. **Incorporate distractions:** Introduce controlled distractions to make the exercise more challenging. Start with little distractions such as low-level noise or a toy, then gradually increase the difficulty. The goal is for your dog to be able to respond to his name despite his disruptive surroundings.
6. **Incorporate movement:** Try moving around while calling your dog's name as you would in real-life scenarios. This helps your dog learn to respond to his name regardless of your location or movement.
7. **Practice in different environments:** Practice this exercise in various locations, including streets, parks, or areas with distractions. This helps the dog generalize the behavior and respond to his name in different settings.
8. **Be consistent:** Stay consistent in using your dog's name and providing rewards for his response. Reinforce the behavior every time he responds promptly to his name, ensuring that he understands the desired outcome.
9. **Gradually withdraw rewards:** Once it has become second nature for your dog to respond to his name, begin to gradually reduce how often you reward him for it. You could switch to intermittent reinforcement so that your dog maintains the behavior without always relying on treats or toys.

Recommended Repetitions

Name Recognition Rally can be practiced in short sessions of 5 to 10 minutes several times a day. You could aim for at least 3 to 5 sessions per week to reinforce the behavior and maintain consistency. And as usual, gradually increase the level of difficulty as your dog becomes more confident and responsive to the commands.

BEAM BALANCE BLISS

Category: Balancing games

Objectives

The Beam Balance Bliss exercise aims to improve a dog's balance, coordination, and body awareness. The objectives of this exercise include enhancing core strength, proprioception, and overall physical stability. Including this exercise in your dog's routine helps build confidence and body control while navigating narrow surfaces.

Description

Beam Balance Bliss is a game that tests your dog's balancing skills and stability. It involves walking or maneuvering on a narrow beam or elevated surface. This exercise promotes body awareness, concentration, and physical control while engaging the dog's muscles in a fun and stimulating way.

How To Perform

1. **Select an appropriate beam or narrow surface:** Choose a sturdy and safe beam or narrow surface for your dog to walk on. It can be a low beam, a wooden plank, or a balance board. Ensure the surface is slip-resistant and provides enough traction for your dog.
2. **Introduce the beam:** Allow your dog to examine the beam or surface without exerting any pressure. Allow him to sniff and inspect it to be familiar with it.
3. **Begin at a low height:** Start with a low surface or beam close to the ground. This will make your dog feel safer and more at ease from the beginning.
4. **Motivate your dog using treats or toys:** Use your dog's favorite treat or toys to encourage him to walk on the beam. Guide him along the beam by holding a treat or favorite toy in front of his nose. Reward him with praise and treats for each successful step.
5. **Gradually increase the difficulty level:** As soon as your dog's confidence grows, gradually increase the beam's height or the surface's narrowness. This will serve as a challenge to his body balance and self-control.
6. **Encourage slow and deliberate movement:** Emphasize slow and deliberate movements to help your dog maintain balance. Encourage him to place each paw carefully on the beam, keeping his body centered and aligned.
7. **Use verbal cues and hand signals:** Introduce verbal cues and hand signals such as "step" or pointing in the direction you want the dog to go. This helps him understand the desired behavior and navigate the beam effectively.
8. **Observe your dog's comfort level:** Pay attention to your dog's body language and comfort level throughout the exercise. If he shows signs of anxiety or stress, reduce the height or widen the surface until he regains confidence.
9. **Gradually increase duration and difficulty:** Gradually increase the duration of the time your dog spends on the beam and introduce more challenging variations, such as turns or stops along the way. This will further develop his body balance and control.

Recommended Repetitions

Start with short sessions of 5 to 10 minutes, and make your primary focus be building your dog's confidence and comfort on the beam. Aim for at least 3 to 5 sessions per week. As your dog progresses, increase the duration of each session and the number of repetitions. Remember to provide breaks and keep the sessions enjoyable and rewarding.

SNUFFLE MAT CHALLENGE

Category: DIY games, Search and scent games

Objectives

The Snuffle Mat Challenge exercise aims to engage your dog's sense of smell and provide mental stimulation through a fun and rewarding game. By using a snuffle mat, whether homemade or purchased, you can encourage your dog to utilize his natural sniffing instincts to search for hidden treats. This activity helps satisfy your dog's mental and sensory needs while promoting focus, problem-solving, and calmness.

Description

Snuffle mats are interactive fabric mats designed to stimulate your dog's sense of smell and provide an engaging and rewarding experience. Whether you choose to make your own snuffle mat or purchase a pre-made one, this exercise will tap into your dog's natural instincts and provide mental enrichment.

What You'll Need:

Option 1 (Homemade Snuffle Mat):
- Sturdy fabric (e.g., fleece, denim, or felt)
- Sewing machine and thread
- Scissors

Option 2 (Purchased Snuffle Mat):
- Plastic mat with a grid of holes (e.g., rubber sink mat)
- Fleece fabric or strips
- Scissors

How To Perform

1. **Homemade snuffle mat:** Cut the sturdy fabric into a square or rectangular shape, depending on your desired size. Use a sewing machine to stitch pockets, flaps, or loops all over the fabric. These will serve as hiding spots for treats. Ensure that the pockets and flaps are securely stitched to prevent treats from falling out too easily. Once completed, your homemade snuffle mat is ready for use.
2. **Purchased snuffle mat:** Choose a plastic mat with a grid of holes, or poke holes in a suitable plastic mat yourself. Tear fleece into strips that are approximately six to eight inches long. Tie a fleece strip through each hole in the mat, creating a "fleece forest" on the top surface. Ensure that the fleece strips are securely tied to the mat.
3. **Hide the treats:** Sprinkle a handful of treats or bits of food onto the surface of the snuffle mat, allowing them to fall into the pockets, flaps, or fleece strips. Ensure that the treats are distributed throughout the mat to provide an enticing and challenging search.
4. **Introduce it to your dog:** Bring your dog to the snuffle mat and let him observe the treats hidden within the fabric. Encourage him to use his sense of smell to locate and retrieve the treats.
5. **Snuffle time:** Give your dog a cue like "Find it!" or "Sniff!" to start the challenge. Watch as your dog snuffles through the fabric, using his nose and paws to uncover the hidden treats. Provide verbal encouragement and praise when your dog successfully finds and retrieves the treats.
6. **Repeat and vary:** Repeat the Snuffle Mat Challenge regularly to keep your dog mentally stimulated. Vary the placement of treats and the complexity of hiding spots to keep the game interesting and challenging for your dog.

Recommended Repetitions

You can engage your dog in the Snuffle Mat Challenge exercise two to three times a week. Adjust the frequency based on your dog's interest and energy level.

FOOD BOWL MANNERS

Category: Impulse control games

Objectives

The Food Bowl Manners exercise aims to teach your dog self-control and polite behavior during mealtime. Other goals of this exercise include promoting calmness, reducing food-guarding behavior, preventing mealtime aggression, and fostering good manners around food.

Description

Food Bowl Manners is a training exercise that focuses on teaching your dog to exhibit calm and polite behavior during mealtime. It involves establishing rules and boundaries around the food bowl and teaching your dog to wait patiently, refrain from rushing or begging, and respect your instructions during feeding time.

How To Perform

1. **Set consistent feeding routines:** Establish a consistent feeding routine for your dog, with set meal times. This helps your dog develop a predictable schedule and reduces anxiety or impulsive behavior around food. Stick to the routine as closely as possible.
2. **Start with basic obedience cues:** Before feeding your dog, ask him to perform basic obedience cues such as sit, stay, or wait. This establishes a foundation of impulse control and sets the tone for polite behavior during mealtime.
3. **Select designated feeding area:** Designate a specific area for your dog's mealtime, preferably away from high-traffic areas or distractions. This helps create a calm and focused environment for your dog to eat without disturbances.
4. **Practice the "Wait" command:** Hold the food bowl and ask your dog to sit or wait patiently before placing the bowl on the ground. Gradually increase the duration of the wait time, rewarding your dog for his patience. This helps reinforce impulse control and teaches him that he must wait for permission to eat.
5. **Encourage calm behavior:** Reinforce calm behavior by rewarding your dog when he exhibits relaxed and polite manners around the food bowl. Offer praise, treats, or gentle petting when he maintains a calm demeanor, avoid rushing, and be patient with him in the feeding process.
6. **Address food guarding behavior:** If your dog displays food guarding behavior, such as growling or snapping when approached near the food bowl, consult with a professional trainer or behaviorist. They can provide guidance on specific exercises to address and manage this behavior safely and effectively.
7. **Consistency is key:** Maintain consistency in your expectations and reinforce the desired behavior consistently. Reinforce good manners during every mealtime, and avoid inadvertently rewarding or reinforcing unwanted behaviors, such as begging or stealing food.

Recommended Repetitions

The Food Bowl Manners exercise should be practiced during each mealtime. Consistency is crucial for establishing good habits and reinforcing polite behavior. Repeat the exercise daily, ensuring that your dog consistently follows the rules and displays good manners around the food bowl.

TOY TAKE AND TRADE

Category: Impulse control games

Objectives

The Toy Take and Trade exercise helps to teach your dog to release toys on cue and engage in a controlled play session. The objectives of this exercise include promoting impulse control, teaching the "take it" and "drop it" commands, and encouraging interactive and rewarding playtime with toys.

Description

Toy Take and Trade is an interactive game that helps develop your dog's impulse control and enhances his ability to engage in controlled play. This exercise involves teaching your dog to take and release toys on command, promoting polite and controlled interactions during playtime.

How To Play

1. **Select suitable toys:** Choose a variety of toys that are safe and suitable for interactive play. Ensure the toys are appealing to your dog and suitable for his size and breed. Use toys with various textures, shapes, and sizes to keep the game interesting and engaging.
2. **Teach the "take it" command:** Begin by presenting a toy to your dog and using the cue "take it." Encourage him to hold the toy in his mouth. When he takes the toy, reward him with praise and a treat. Repeat this step several times to reinforce the association between the cue and the action of taking the toy.
3. **Teach the "drop it" command:** Once your dog has a good grasp of the "take it" command, introduce the "drop it" command. Hold a treat in your hand and show it to your dog. Say the word "drop it" and offer the treat as a trade for the toy they have in their mouth. When your dog releases the toy, reward him with the treat.
4. **Practice the toy exchange:** Encourage your dog to engage in playful interaction with the toy by using exciting and animated movements. After a short play session, give the cue "drop it" and offer a treat as a trade for the toy. Repeat this exchange during playtime to reinforce the concept of releasing the toy in exchange for a reward.
5. **Gradually increase difficulty:** As your dog gets better at taking and releasing toys on cue, gradually increase the difficulty level. Introduce distractions or create scenarios where your dog needs to exhibit self-control and wait for the cue before taking or releasing the toy. This will help reinforce impulse control and obedience.
6. **Engage in interactive play:** Use the Toy Take and Trade exercise as an opportunity to engage in interactive play sessions with your dog. Encourage him to chase, tug, and interact with the toys. Hence, using this as an avenue to reinforce positive behaviors and redirect any inappropriate behaviors.

Recommended Repetitions

Practice the Toy Take and Trade exercise during regular play sessions. Start with short sessions of 5 to 10 minutes a few times a week, and gradually increase the duration and frequency as your dog becomes proficient in the exercise. Aim for multiple repetitions during each session, focusing on reinforcing the "take it" and "drop it" commands.

SPLASH AND RETRIEVE

Category: Water and diving games

Objectives

The Splash and Retrieve exercise engages your dog in water-based play and retrieve activities. Objectives of this exercise include building confidence in the water, improving swimming skills, enhancing retrieving abilities, and providing a fun and refreshing outlet for physical and mental stimulation.

Description

Splash and Retrieve is a water-based game that blends swimming and retrieving skills. This exercise provides an enjoyable way for dogs to cool down, exercise, and have fun in the water. It involves throwing a floating toy into the water for your dog to retrieve, promoting their natural instincts and providing mental and physical stimulation.

How To Play

1. **Select a suitable water environment:** Choose a safe and suitable environment for your dog to participate in this exercise. It can be a pool, a calm lake, or a dog-friendly beach with shallow and calm waters. Ensure the area is free from hazards and provides ample space for your dog to swim and retrieve.
2. **Introduce the floating toy:** Find a floating toy that is safe for water play, such as a buoyant ball or a floating disc. Introduce the toy to your dog and let him get familiar with it on land before moving to the water.
3. **Encourage your dog to enter the water:** If your dog is new to swimming or hesitant about entering the water, you can encourage him by using positive reinforcement techniques. Start by wading into the water yourself and calling your dog to join you. Offer treats and praise as he gradually enters the water and becomes comfortable.
4. **Toss the toy into the water:** Once your dog is comfortable in the water, throw the floating toy a short distance into the water and close to the shoreline. Use an enthusiastic and positive tone to motivate your dog to swim and retrieve the toy.
5. **Celebrate successful retrieves:** When your dog swims to the toy and retrieves it, celebrate his success with praise, treats, and positive reinforcement. Repeat the process and gradually increase the distance of the throws as your dog becomes more confident and skilled.
6. **Pay close attention to the exercise:** While your dog is engaged in Splash and Retrieve, ensure you are there to provide close supervision and monitor his safety at all times. Avoid areas with strong currents, deep waters, or hazardous conditions. Pay attention to your dog's energy levels and take breaks as needed to prevent exhaustion.

Recommended Repetitions

The Splash and Retrieve exercise can be repeated for several sessions, depending on your dog's water proficiency and stamina. Starting with shorter sessions allows your dog to gradually build endurance and retrieving skills. Also, be mindful of your dog's comfort level and physical condition, ensuring he is not overexerted during the exercise.

HIDDEN TREATS HUNT

Category: Search and scent games

Objectives

The Hidden Treats Hunt exercise is designed to enhance your dog's impulse control and focus while engaging in a fun and rewarding game. By hiding treats under your dog's favorite toys and teaching him to wait for your cue, this exercise promotes patience, obedience, and mental stimulation. It strengthens the bond between you and your dog while providing an opportunity for interactive play.

Description

The exciting Hidden Treats Hunt is an interactive game you can play indoors with your dog. By hiding treats under his toys and teaching him to wait for your signal, you'll create an engaging activity that challenges your dog's impulse control and enhances his cognitive skills.

How To Play

1. **Gather toys and treats:** Collect several of your dog's favorite toys. Prepare a variety of small treats that will fit under the toys.
2. **Prepare for the game:** Have your dog sit and watch you as you hide treats under his toys. Make sure your dog remains calm and focused during this preparation phase.
3. **Hide the treats:** Place treats under different toys while your dog observes. Vary the difficulty level by hiding treats in different locations or using different toys each time you play.
4. **Use a verbal cue:** Once you have hidden the treats, use a specific verbal cue, such as "Now" or "Search!" Encourage your dog to start searching for the treats using an enthusiastic and excited tone.
5. **Reward and praise:** As your dog discovers a treat under a toy, praise him with excitement and provide immediate rewards. Use verbal cues like "Good job!" or offer additional treats to reinforce his success.
6. **Repeat and vary the game:** Continue playing the game, hiding treats under different toys each time to keep it challenging and engaging. Celebrate your dog's progress and reward him for his patience and obedience during the waiting phase.

Important Tips:

- Choose toys that are safe and suitable for your dog's size and breed.
- Use small, dog-friendly treats that easily fit under the toys.
- Monitor your dog closely during the game to prevent him from accidentally ingesting non-edible parts of the toys.
- Make the game enjoyable and rewarding for your dog by providing praise, treats, and positive reinforcement.

Recommended Repetitions

The Hidden Treats Hunt game can be played everyday depending on your dog's energy level and mood. It is a good way to get him engaged with the right dose of daily mental and physical stimulation, also reinforcing good behaviors such as patience, impulse control, and obedience.

MIND-MAZING MAZE

Category: Intelligence and brain games (IQ games)

Objectives

The Mind-Mazing Maze exercise is designed to challenge your dog's problem-solving abilities, enhance his cognitive skills, and provide mental stimulation. The objectives of this exercise include promoting focus and concentration, improving decision-making skills, enhancing spatial awareness, and engaging your dog's problem-solving capabilities.

Description

The Mind-Mazing Maze is an interactive and mentally-stimulating game that requires your dog to navigate through a maze or obstacle course to reach a desired goal. This exercise encourages your dog to think critically, make strategic decisions, and overcome obstacles to successfully complete the maze. It provides an engaging and rewarding experience that exercises his mind while promoting focus and mental agility.

How To Play

1. **Set up the maze:** Create a maze or set up an obstacle course using various objects, such as cones, chairs, tunnels, or other items. Design a layout that offers your dog different paths and challenges to navigate.
2. **Choose a starting point and goal:** Determine a clear starting point and a designated goal within the maze. You can use treats, toys, or other rewards as the desired goal to motivate your dog.
3. **Introduce the maze:** Allow your dog to get familiar with the maze or obstacle course. Guide him through the initial paths, demonstrating how to navigate the obstacles and reach the goal. You may use treats or favorite toys as rewards during the introduction phase to help your dog create a positive association with the maze.
4. **Encourage problem-solving:** Gradually increase the difficulty level by introducing barriers, dead-ends, or additional challenges within the maze. This pushes your dog to problem-solve, analyze different paths, and make decisions on how to reach the goal.
5. Allow verbal cues and guidance: Use verbal cues like "Find the way" or "Through the maze" to guide your dog's attention and direct him towards the correct path. Be sure to provide encouragement and positive reinforcement as he makes progress or overcomes obstacles.
6. **Reward successful efforts:** When your dog successfully navigates through the maze and reaches the goal, follow up with immediate and enthusiastic praise. Offer treats, play, or other rewards to reinforce his accomplishment and as a motivation to always be engaged in the game.
7. **Increase complexity and variety:** As your dog begins to ace the challenge and complete the maze in a shorter time, gradually increase the complexity by adding more obstacles, changing the layout, or introducing different challenges. Gradually increasing the complexity of the exercise makes it engaging and provides ongoing mental stimulation for your dog.

Recommended Repetitions

The Mind-Mazing Maze exercise can be repeated several times a week, depending on your dog's interest and energy level. Start with shorter sessions and simpler mazes. Slowly but surely, gradually increase the duration and complexity as your dog becomes more skilled. Aim for multiple repetitions per session to ensure your dog remains engaged and challenged throughout the exercise.

CARDBOARD TREAT HUNTER

Category: Search and scent games, DIY games

Objectives

The Cardboard Treat Hunter exercise aims to stimulate your dog's problem-solving skills, encourage mental engagement, and provide an exciting treasure hunt experience. By using cardboard containers as treat dispensers, your dog will engage his senses, improve focus, and enjoy the challenge of retrieving delicious rewards.

Description

Unleash your dog's inner detective with the Cardboard Treat Hunter exercise. This interactive game involves using simple household materials to create treat-filled puzzles that will keep your dog entertained and mentally sharp.

How To Play

1. **Gather materials:** You'll need the following materials:
   - Empty toilet paper tubes or paper towel rolls
   - Soft treats (e.g., peanut butter or cream cheese)
   - Optional: Hard dog treats or kibble
   - Empty box with a sealable top
   - Utility knife or scissors
   - Supervision during playtime
2. **Create the destructible tube treat dispenser:** Take an empty toilet paper tube or paper towel roll and stuff it with soft treats. Your dog will need to lick and manipulate the tube to access the treats, preventing it from rolling away. For an increased challenge, fold down the ends of the tube, encouraging your dog to tear into the cardboard to reach the goodies inside. Remember to remove any small pieces of cardboard that may come off during play to prevent ingestion.
3. **Treat-filled box challenge:** If your dog prefers hard treats or kibble, use an empty box instead. Poke holes in the box that are slightly larger than the size of the treats. Place the treats inside the box and seal the top securely. Your dog will need to toss and manipulate the box to make the treats fall out through the holes. Vary the challenge by using different sizes and types of containers, such as a cylindrical potato chip tube or a pizza box.
4. **Playtime:** Introduce the treat dispensers to your dog and allow him to explore and sniff. Encourage your dog to engage with the cardboard puzzles using a playful and enthusiastic tone. Provide praise and rewards when your dog successfully retrieves the treats from the containers. Monitor your dog to ensure he doesn't consume any non-edible parts of the cardboard.
5. **Increase the difficulty:** As your dog becomes proficient at solving the puzzles, make it more challenging. Increase the number of treat dispensers or hide them in trickier spots. Introduce new techniques, such as freezing the treat-filled tube or box before offering it to your dog for a longer-lasting challenge.

Safety Precautions:

- Always supervise your dog during playtime with cardboard treat dispensers.
- Use dog-friendly treats and check for any allergies or dietary restrictions.
- Remove any small pieces of cardboard that may pose a choking hazard.

Recommended Repetitions

Engage in the Cardboard Treat Hunter exercise for 10 to 15 minutes per session a few times a week. Adjust the duration based on your dog's energy level and attention span.

TREASURE BOX SNIFFER

Category: Search and scent games, DIY games, Indoor games

Objectives

The "Cardboard Treat Hunter" exercise aims to stimulate your dog's problem-solving skills, encourage mental engagement, and provide an exciting treasure hunt experience. By using cardboard containers as treat dispensers, your dog will engage their senses, improve focus, and enjoy the challenge of retrieving delicious rewards.

Description

Treasure Box Sniffer' is a delightful indoor scent activity designed to engage your dog's senses and challenge his problem-solving abilities. This game involves setting up a group of empty containers, like shoe boxes or yogurt tubs, and strategically hiding treats in some of them. As your dog enters the room, his keen sense of smell will guide him to search for the hidden treasures among the boxes. This interactive game strengthens the bond between you and your dog while tapping into his natural instincts, making it an enjoyable and rewarding experience for both of you.

How To Play

1. **Gather materials:** Collect several empty containers, such as shoe boxes or yogurt tubs. Ensure the containers are clean and safe for your dog to interact with.
2. **Set up the game:** Place the empty containers in a group on the floor, ensuring they are spaced apart. Bait one or a few containers with pleasant-smelling treats while leaving the rest empty.
3. **Hide the treasure:** With your dog in another room or temporarily distracted, place the treats inside the selected containers. Vary the difficulty level by placing treats in different containers each time you play.
4. **Start the search:** Bring your dog into the room with the containers and let him sniff and explore. Encourage your dog to search by using an excited and enthusiastic tone.
5. **Finding the treats:** As your dog investigates the containers, praise and reward him when he discovers a treat. Allow your dog to eat the treat as a reward for his successful find.
6. **Progression and challenge:** Continue playing the game, gradually increasing the difficulty by using more containers or hiding treats in trickier spots. Celebrate your dog's progress and provide ample praise and rewards for each successful find.
7. **Ending the game:** Once your dog has found all the hidden treats, lure him away from the search area using a treat in your hand. Praise your dog and give him the lure treat to signal the end of the game.

Important Tips:

- Always use safe and dog-friendly treats for the game.
- Monitor your dog closely during the exercise to ensure he does not accidentally ingest any non-edible parts of the containers.
- Keep the game exciting and enjoyable for your dog by varying the placement of treats and introducing new hiding spots.

Recommended Repetitions

The Treasure Box Sniffer game can be played for approximately 10 to 15 minutes per session a few times a week. Adjust the duration based on your dog's energy level and attention span.

MINDFULNESS MOMENTS

Category: Mental health games

Objectives

Mindfulness Moments is an exercise that promotes mental well-being and relaxation for you and your dog. The objectives of this exercise include fostering a sense of calmness, reducing stress and anxiety, increasing focus and attention, improving emotional regulation, and strengthening the bond between you and your dog.

Description

Mindfulness Moments involves creating a peaceful and mindful environment where you and your dog can engage in calming activities together. This exercise aims to cultivate a state of presence and awareness, allowing you and your dog to relax, de-stress, and connect on a deeper level. Mindfulness activities can include gentle touch, breathing exercises, visualization, and sensory stimulation.

How to Perform

1. **Choose a quiet and comfortable space:** Find a calm and quiet area where you and your dog can relax without distractions. It could be a cozy corner in your home, a serene outdoor location, or a designated mindfulness area.
2. **Practice deep breathing:** Sit or lie down next to your dog and begin by taking slow, deep breaths. Encourage your dog to do the same by observing his natural breathing patterns. This helps both of you relax and enter a more mindful state.
3. **Engage in gentle touch:** Pet your dog gently and focus on the sensations of touch. Observe the texture of his fur, the warmth of his body, and the connection between your hand and his skin. This helps create a calming and soothing experience for both of you.
4. **Incorporate sensory stimulation:** Introduce elements of sensory stimulation, like soft music, aromatic scents, or gentle sounds. These can enhance the relaxation experience and engage your dog's senses in a positive way.
5. **Maintain a mindful presence:** Focus on being present with your dog throughout the exercise. Be attentive to his reactions, body language, and the connection you share. Avoid rushing or forcing any particular outcome—simply embrace the present moment together.

Recommended Repetitions

Mindfulness Moments can be practiced as often as desired, depending on your and your dog's needs. You can engage in these exercises daily or incorporate them into your routine whenever you or your dog could benefit from relaxation and mental rejuvenation. Each session can last between 5 to 15 minutes, but you may adjust the duration based on your dog's comfort and engagement level.

CARDBOARD TRAIN

Category: Search and scent games, DIY games

Objectives

The Cardboard Train game aims to stimulate your dog's sense of smell, encourage problem-solving, and provide mental enrichment. This interactive exercise engages his natural sniffing instincts, promotes focus and concentration, and rewards his efforts in finding hidden treats. It also strengthens the bond between you and your dog through positive reinforcement and encouragement.

Description

Cardboard Train is an engaging game that combines scent detection and problem-solving. By using a simple setup of empty boxes, toilet rolls, and a scarf, you can create a challenging puzzle for your dog to solve. This game encourages him to use his nose to search for hidden treats and rewards his curiosity and persistence.

How to Perform

1. **Prepare the fame setup:** For this, you'll need the following materials:
   - Empty boxes, cartons, and cardboard
   - Toilet rolls or kitchen roll tubes
   - Treats
   - An old scarf
2. **Prepare the sniffing circle:** Take one end of the scarf and pass it into one end of the toilet roll, making it come out of the other end. Repeat this process with multiple toilet rolls, connecting them to create a circular shape. Tie both ends of the scarf together to form a secure knot, ensuring the toilet rolls are held in place.
3. **Hide the treats:** Place treats in between the scarf and the toilet rolls, ensuring they are securely held and won't easily fall off. Distribute the treats evenly around the circle, creating a challenging and enticing search area.
4. **Introduce the game:** Let your dog have a look at the Cardboard Train and get familiar with the scent of the hidden treats. Encourage your dog to sniff around the scarf and the toilet rolls, using a happy and enthusiastic tone.
5. **Sniffing and discovering:** Watch as your dog uses his nose to search for the hidden treats within the Sniffing Circle. Provide positive reinforcement and support when needed, praising and rewarding your dog for each successful find.
6. **Adjust and vary the challenge:** As your dog becomes more skilled at finding the treats, you can increase the difficulty by adding more layers of scarf and toilet rolls. Keep the game engaging by varying the placement of treats and introducing new hiding spots.
7. **Enjoy the fun:** Celebrate his successes and cherish the special bond you share while playing this interactive game together.

Recommended Repetitions

The frequency and duration of the Cardboard Train game can vary depending on your dog's individual needs and preferences. Start with shorter play sessions of about 5 to10 minutes and gradually increase the duration as your dog becomes more skilled at finding treats. Incorporate this game into your dog's routine a few times per week to provide mental stimulation and keep his sniffing skills sharp.

SOLO PLAYTIME SURPRISE

Category: Left alone games

Objectives

Solo Playtime Surprise is an engaging exercise designed to provide mental stimulation and entertainment for your dog during alone time. The objective of this exercise is to encourage independent play, alleviate boredom, and prevent destructive behaviors that may arise from separation anxiety or lack of mental stimulation.

Description

Solo Playtime Surprise involves setting up a stimulating environment for your dog to explore and interact with various toys and mentally-enriching activities while you're away. The aim is to create an enjoyable experience that keeps your dog mentally engaged and entertained during his alone time.

How to Perform

1. **Create a safe space:** Set up a designated area or room where your dog can have his solo playtime. Ensure the space is dog-proofed, free from hazards, and comfortable for your dog.
2. **Select the toys:** Choose a variety of interactive toys, puzzle toys, treat-dispensing toys, and chew toys that are safe and suitable for your dog's size, age, and play preferences. Ensure the toys are durable and capable of challenging your dog on different levels.
3. **Vary the toys:** Shuffle the toys regularly to maintain novelty and keep your dog interested. This prevents boredom and helps sustain his engagement during solo playtime sessions.
4. **Provide enrichment activities:** These are activities that stimulate your dog's senses and engage his problem-solving skills. Examples include hiding treats or toys in puzzle toys, freezing treats in ice cubes, or using food-dispensing balls.
5. **Introduce surprise elements:** Incorporating surprises makes solo playtime more exciting. This can be done by hiding toys in different locations, using interactive toys that make sounds or move unpredictably, or including scents or food puzzles that require a little bit of searching.
6. **Establish a routine:** Gradually introduce solo playtime to your dog by starting with shorter durations and gradually increasing the length as they become more comfortable. Use positive reinforcement, such as treats or praise, to create a positive association with this exercise.

Recommended Repetitions

Solo Playtime Surprise can be incorporated into your dog's daily routine, especially during periods of alone time. Aim for at least one solo playtime session per day, lasting anywhere from 15 to 30 minutes, depending on your dog's energy level and attention span. Also, try to adjust the duration and frequency based on your dog's needs.

STUFFED KONG

Category: Mental health games, Food games

Objectives

The Stuffed Kong exercise aims to provide mental stimulation, promote problem-solving skills, and offer a rewarding experience for your dog. By filling a Kong toy with a variety of treats and food, you can keep him engaged, entertained, and mentally challenged.

Description

The Stuffed Kong exercise involves filling a Kong toy with a delicious mixture of treats and food. It encourages your dog to work for his rewards by using his problem-solving abilities and keeping him mentally stimulated.

How to Perform

1. **Select your toy:** Start by selecting a Kong toy suitable for your dog's size and chewing strength.
2. **Gather adequate treats:** Gather a selection of treats and food items that your dog enjoys, such as peanut butter, mashed banana, yogurt, diced fruits or vegetables, and dry kibble.
3. **Close the toy:** Plug the small hole at the bottom of the Kong with a larger treat or piece of kibble.
4. Stuff with chosen filling: Fill the Kong with the stuffing mixture, making sure to pack it tightly to provide a greater challenge for your dog.
5. **Create surprises:** Add larger treats or pieces of food intermittently throughout the stuffing to create surprises and increase engagement.
6. **Close the toy:** Seal the top opening of the Kong with a spread of peanut butter or a larger treat.
7. **Present to your dog:** Present the stuffed Kong to your dog and let him enjoy the process of extracting the treats from the toy.
8. **Vary it:** You can offer the stuffed Kong to your dog as-is or freeze it for a longer-lasting and more challenging experience.
9. **Do not forget to keep an eye on him:** Supervise your dog during playtime and remove any small or loose pieces that may pose a choking hazard.

Recommended Repetitions

The Stuffed Kong exercise can be incorporated into your dog's routine as a regular mental enrichment activity. It can be done multiple times a week or as often as you see fit to keep your dog mentally stimulated and entertained.

ZEN ZONE TRAINING

Category: Mental health games

Objectives

Zen Zone Training is a mental health game that focuses on teaching your dog to find inner calmness and develop self-control. The objective of this exercise is to help your dog achieve a state of relaxation, promote mental clarity, and improve his ability to self-soothe in stressful situations.

Description

Zen Zone Training involves creating a designated space where your dog can go to relax and find tranquility. This exercise aims to provide a safe and peaceful environment for your dog to unwind and practice self-calming techniques.

How to Perform

1. **Create a designated zen zone:** Select a specific area in your home or yard that will serve as the Zen Zone. This space should be quiet, free from distractions, and comfortable for your dog.
2. **Make the zen zone relaxing:** This can be achieved by adding soft bedding, calming scents, and gentle lighting. Play soft, soothing music or use a white noise machine to create a peaceful ambiance.
3. **Introduce the cue:** Teach your dog a specific cue or command that signals it's time to enter the Zen Zone. For example, you can use "Zen" or "Relax." You could also associate these cues with positive reinforcement to motivate your dog to get into the Zen Zone.
4. **Practice relaxation exercises:** Encourage your dog to enter the Zen Zone on command. Guide him to lie down or settle on the comfortable bedding. Gradually introduce relaxation exercises, such as deep breathing or progressive muscle relaxation, to help him achieve a state of calmness.
5. **Extend zen zone time:** Start with short durations in the Zen Zone, and gradually increase the time as your dog becomes more comfortable. Encourage him to remain relaxed and reward him for maintaining a calm and composed state.
6. **Generalize the behavior:** Once your dog understands the concept of the Zen Zone, start incorporating it into various situations, such as during visitors' arrival, in noisy environments, or before potentially stressful events. This helps your dog develop the ability to connect with his Zen state even in challenging circumstances.

Recommended Repetitions

Consistency is crucial for Zen Zone Training to be effective. Practice this exercise daily, and gradually increase the duration of Zen Zone sessions. Start with short intervals of 5 to 10 minutes and work your way up to 30 minutes or longer, depending on your dog's comfort level and ability to relax. Incorporating Zen Zone Training into your dog's routine can provide valuable mental health benefits, allowing him to navigate stressful situations more easily and maintain a sense of inner peace. Through consistent practice and positive reinforcement, you can help your dog find his Zen Zone and cultivate a calm and balanced state of mind.

MENTAL EXERCISE INTERMEDIATE LEVEL

Welcome to the Intermediate Level of mentally-stimulating exercises for dogs! I hope it has been an interesting journey for you and your dog. At this stage, you and your beloved pet have mastered the basics and are ready to take his (i.e., your dog's) mental abilities and physical skills to the next level.

Intermediate exercises provide a greater challenge, which would require your dog to think more strategically, display improved focus, and demonstrate increased control over his impulses. These exercises build upon the foundation laid at the Basic Level and offer an exciting opportunity for further growth and development.

At this level, you can expect exercises that promote problem-solving, advanced obedience, and enhanced coordination. Get ready for a fulfilling part of your journey where you'll witness your dog's progress and see him put his mental prowess to work!

SEEK AND SPEAK

Category: Search and scent games, Intelligence and brain games

Objectives

The Seek and Speak exercise is designed to enhance your dog's listening skills and strengthen the unique communication between you and your dog. By using verbal cues and vocal tones, this game encourages your dog to locate a hidden treat or toy while reinforcing his ability to interpret different tones of voice. Through this interactive activity, you'll foster a deeper bond with your dog and stimulate is mental engagement.

Description

The Seek and Speak exercise is an exciting treasure hunt you can embark on with your pet. By utilizing verbal communication and vocal tones, you'll guide your dog to find hidden treats or toys while strengthening your shared language.

How to Play

1. **Prepare the game:** Choose a treat or toy that your dog finds enticing and hide it in a location where your dog cannot see or access it. Ensure it's a safe and suitable hiding spot. Make sure your dog is not observing the hiding process to maintain the element of surprise.
2. **Start the game:** Begin by calmly telling your dog to stay or have someone hold him gently to prevent him from peeking or searching prematurely. Use a calm and neutral tone of voice as you announce, "Find it" or "Search."
3. **Hide and seek:** Place the treat or toy in the chosen hiding spot while your dog is not watching. Release your dog and encourage him to start searching by saying, "Find it," or using a specific command you have trained him to associate with searching.
4. **Verbal cues:** As your dog explores, use a calm and gentle tone of voice, saying, "Colder" if he moves away from the hidden treat or toy. This indicates that he is farther from the target. Switch to a more excited and enthusiastic tone saying, "Hotter" as your dog gets closer to the hidden treat or toy.
5. **Finding the treasure:** Continue providing verbal cues, alternating between "Colder" and "Hotter" based on your dog's proximity to the hidden item. Once your dog discovers the treat or toy, celebrate his success with praise and excitement. Reward your dog with the treat or allow him to enjoy playing with the toy as a well-deserved prize.
6. **Repeat and reinforce:** Play multiple rounds of Seek and Speak to reinforce your dog's listening skills and his understanding of vocal cues. Vary the hiding spots and difficulty level to keep the game challenging and engaging for your dog.

Recommended Repetitions

Engage in the "Seek and Speak" exercise for about 10 to 15 minutes per session. Repeat the game a few times a week to maintain mental stimulation and strengthen the bond between you and your dog.

THE WHICH HAND GAME

Category: Focus games

Objectives

The Which Hand Game is designed to enhance your dog's focus, concentration, and ability to make decisions based on visual and olfactory cues. This exercise encourages mental stimulation and strengthens the bond between you and your dog. By playing the Which Hand Game, your dog will develop his ability to discriminate scents and make informed choices.

Description

The Which Hand Game is a fun and interactive exercise that challenges your dog's cognitive abilities. In this game, you will use treats and your hands to engage your dog's senses and stimulate his mental faculties. By practicing this game regularly, your dog will become more adept at detecting scent cues and making accurate choices.

How to Play

1. **Prepare treats:** Start by gathering a handful of small, bite-sized treats that your dog finds enticing.
2. **Sit position:** Have your dog sit in front of you and maintain a calm and focused demeanor.
3. **Treat placement:** Take one treat and place it in one of your hands. Close your hands into a downward facing fist, ensuring that your dog cannot see or smell the treat.
4. **Present hands:** Extend your closed fists towards your dog, with your palms facing downwards. Hold your hands at a comfortable distance from your dog's nose, allowing him to sniff the scents coming from your hands.
5. **Ask "Which hand?":** Using a clear and enthusiastic tone, ask your dog, "Which hand?" or any other verbal cue that you prefer.
6. **Let your dog choose:** Observe your dog's behavior and body language closely. Encourage him to use his sense of smell and visual observation to determine which hand holds the treat.
7. **Reveal the treat:** Once your dog makes a choice by sniffing or pawing at a hand, open the corresponding hand to reveal whether he has selected the correct one.
8. **Reward and repeat:** If your dog chooses the correct hand, praise him and reward him with the treat. If he chooses incorrectly, calmly show him the empty hand and withhold the treat. Repeat the process, varying the hand in which you hide the treat each time.

Recommended Repetitions

The Which Hand Game can be played for short sessions of 5 to 10 minutes, a few times a week. It's important to keep the game fun and engaging without overloading your dog's cognitive abilities. As your dog becomes more skilled at the game, you can gradually increase the difficulty by using more challenging hiding techniques or introducing distractions. Remember to adjust the frequency and duration of the game based on your dog's individual needs and energy levels.

SPIN THE BOTTLE

Category: DIY games, Intelligence and brain games, Indoor games

Objectives

Spin the Bottle is a fun and engaging DIY exercise designed to provide mental stimulation and entertainment for your dog. This exercise promotes problem-solving skills, coordination, and focus. By interacting with the spinning bottle, your dog will work to access the treats inside, enhancing his cognitive abilities and providing a mentally enriching experience.

Description

Spin the Bottle is an indoor DIY game that involves creating a treat dispensing bottle with two holes on opposite sides. A thread is passed through the holes and held by two doors or other stable objects, suspending the bottle in the middle. Treats are placed inside the bottle, enticing your dog to engage in the interactive play.

What You'll Need

- Clean, empty plastic bottle
- Utility knife or scissors (to create holes in the bottle)
- A thick, strong thread (to pass through the holes in the bottle)
- Small treats or kibble

How to Perform

1. **Prepare the bottle:** Take an empty plastic bottle and clean it thoroughly, ensuring it is free from any residual liquid or debris. Remove labels or stickers from the bottle and let it dry completely.
2. **Create treat openings:** Using a utility knife or scissors, carefully make two holes on opposite sides of the bottle. The holes should be large enough for treats to fall out when the bottle spins. Place the holes near the middle of the bottle for balanced suspension.
3. **Thread the bottle:** Pass a strong and durable thread through one hole and out the other, ensuring the bottle is securely suspended in the middle. Tie knots on both ends of the thread to prevent it from slipping out.
4. **Secure the thread:** Attach the ends of the thread to two doors or any stable objects at a suitable height for your dog to interact with the spinning bottle. Make sure the doors are securely closed, keeping the bottle suspended and accessible to your dog.
5. **Fill the bottle with treats:** Unscrew the bottle cap or remove the top and fill the bottle with your dog's favorite treats. Ensure the treats are small enough to easily come out of the holes when the bottle is spun.
6. **Introduce Spin the bottle:** Guide your dog to the suspended bottle and encourage him to investigate. Show him how to interact with the bottle by using his nose or paw to spin it. As the bottle spins, treats will be released through the holes, rewarding your dog's effort.
7. **Encourage and reinforce:** Offer praise and positive reinforcement when your dog successfully spins the bottle and retrieves the treats. Celebrate his efforts and make the experience enjoyable for them.
8. **Supervise and adjust:** Keep an eye on your dog during the game to ensure his safety. If the thread or bottle becomes damaged or shows signs of wear and tear, replace them promptly. Adjust the difficulty level as needed by changing the size of the treat openings or introducing more challenging ways to spin the bottle.

Note

Always monitor your dog while playing this game and ensure he doesn't chew on the bottle or ingest any non-edible parts. Adjust the game to your dog's individual needs and preferences, making it a fun and interactive experience for them.

Recommended Repetitions

Engage your dog in the Spin the Bottle exercise for short sessions, around 5 to 10 minutes, a few times per week. Regular and consistent play will help maintain your dog's interest and provide ongoing mental stimulation.

FLYING DISC FRENZY

Category: Outdoor games, Focus games, Agility games

Objectives

The Flying Disc Frenzy exercise aims to provide physical exercise and mental stimulation and enhance the bond between you and your dog through the exciting game of fetch using a flying disc. The objective is to improve your dog's agility, coordination, and focus while engaging in an enjoyable outdoor activity.

Description

Flying Disc Frenzy is a high-energy game that combines exercise and mental stimulation for your dog. It involves throwing a flying disc or Frisbee and encouraging your dog to chase, catch, and retrieve it. This is an intermediate-level exercise suitable for dogs who enjoy playing fetch and have the physical capability to jump and run.

How to Perform

1. **Select an appropriate disc:** Choose a flying disc that is designed for dogs. Look for a disc made of durable material that is safe for your dog's teeth and easy to throw. Avoid discs with sharp edges or those made of hard plastic, as they may cause injury to your dog.
2. **Choose a space for the exercise:** Find an open, safe area, such as a park or a spacious backyard, where you can play the game without any obstructions or hazards. Ensure there is enough space for your dog to run freely and chase the disc.
3. **Start with a warm-up:** Engage your dog in a short warm-up session to prevent any muscle strain or injuries. You can do some light stretching exercises or play a brief game of tug-of-war to get your muscles fired up.
4. **Demonstrate proper throwing technique:** Hold the flying disc flat in your hand and use an overhand throwing motion to launch it into the air. Aim for a straight and level throw to make it easier for your dog to catch.
5. **Encourage chase and retrieve:** As you throw the disc, use an excited and encouraging tone to prompt your dog to chase after it. When your dog catches the disc, reward him with praise and possibly a treat. Encourage him to bring the disc back to you for another throw.
6. **Increase difficulty level:** Start with short and easy throws, and gradually increase the distance as your dog becomes more comfortable and proficient. You can also make the catches a bit challenging by throwing the disc higher or making it spin in the air.

Recommended Repetitions

The Flying Disc Frenzy exercise can be enjoyed in short sessions to avoid overexertion. Aim for 10 to 15 minutes of playtime per session, depending on your dog's fitness level and stamina. Take breaks between throws to allow your dog to rest and hydrate. Repeat the exercise a few times per week to maintain physical and mental stimulation.

STEADY AS A ROCK

Category: Balancing games

Objectives

The Steady as a Rock exercise aims to improve your dog's balance, stability, and body awareness. Key areas that this exercise targets include strengthening core muscles, enhancing coordination, and promoting your dog's overall stability and fitness.

Description

Steady as a Rock is a balancing exercise designed to challenge your dog's balance control. It involves teaching your dog to maintain a stable position on various objects or unstable surfaces. This exercise can build strength, stability, and body control while engaging your dog's mind and body.

How to Perform

1. **Choose a stable object:** Select a stable object-balance disc, stable rock, or wobble board suitable for your dog's size and ability. Ensure the object is safe for your dog to stand on.
2. **Introduce the object:** Stay calm and positive as you introduce the object to your dog. Allow your dog to sniff and explore the object to familiarize himself with it. Also, encourage his curiosity and create a positive association with the object by offering treats and praises.
3. **Start with a stable surface:** Begin the exercise on a stable surface like the floor or a sturdy platform. Let your dog be on all four paws on the object, and reward him for maintaining his balance. Gradually increase the duration of his stay on the object to reinforce the desired behavior.
4. **Progress to unstable surfaces:** Once your dog is comfortable on a stable surface, gradually introduce more challenging and unstable surfaces as they require more effort and body control to maintain balance.
5. **Incorporate verbal cues and hand signals:** Teach your dog verbal cues and hand signals to indicate the desired behavior. For example, you can use the word "steady" together with a hand signal to encourage your dog to maintain his balance. Ensure to remain consistent in your cues and signals to help your dog understand and respond appropriately.
6. **Gradually increase the difficulty:** Once your dog becomes more balanced, you increase the difficulty level by introducing additional challenges like asking him to shift his weight from one paw to another, performing simple movements or tricks while maintaining balance, or introducing distractions to test their focus.
7. **Celebrate and reinforce:** Celebrate your dog's efforts and achievements and use positive reinforcement techniques such as treats, praise, or warm petting to reward him.

Recommended Repetitions

The number of repetitions and practice sessions depends on your dog's fitness level, balance, and coordination. Start with shorter sessions of 5 to 10 minutes, a few times per week, and gradually increase the exercise time and frequency as your dog becomes more proficient. Anywhere from 5 to 10 repetitions per session is okay, but make sure to focus on the quality of the exercise and engagement with your dog.

TEACH AND SHOW OFF

Category: Kids games

Objectives

Teach and Show Off is an exercise that promotes mental stimulation, confidence, and a sense of achievement in both children and dogs. This exercise allows children to actively participate in teaching dogs a few impressive tricks or skills, fostering a stronger bond and a sense of responsibility. This process of teaching helps both the child and the dog to grow mentally, improve their focus, and allow for more cooperation between both parties.

Description

Teach and Show Off involves children taking an active role in teaching their dog complex tricks or advanced behaviors. It encourages children to become responsible trainers, enhancing their communication skills and promoting a sense of pride in their achievements. This game offers an opportunity for both the child and the dog to learn and demonstrate impressive skills together.

How to Perform

1. **Select desired behaviors:** You and your children are to choose a set of advanced tricks or behaviors that you would like to teach your dog. These could include complex tricks like rolling over, playing dead, jumping through hoops, or any other exciting behaviors they want to showcase.
2. **Break It down:** Break each behavior into smaller, manageable steps that are easy for the children and the dog to understand. Demonstrate and explain each step clearly, encouraging the kids to actively participate in the teaching process.
3. **Reward-based training:** You and your children are to choose a set of advanced tricks or behaviors that you would like to teach your dog. These could include complex tricks like rolling over, playing dead, jumping through hoops, or any other exciting behaviors they want to showcase.
4. **Practice and refine:** Practice each behavior regularly, allowing the children to take the lead in training sessions. Encourage them to be patient and consistent, guiding the dog through each step and providing positive reinforcement. Also, make the practice sessions fun and interactive to foster a joyful learning environment.
5. **Show off:** Once your dog has mastered the behaviors, it's time for the kids to showcase their training skills. Invite family and friends, or even host a mini-performance to demonstrate the impressive tricks they have taught the dog. Encourage your children to be proud of their accomplishments and celebrate their achievements.

Recommended Repetitions

The repetition of Teach and Show Off will depend on the complexity of the behaviors being taught. Encourage your children to engage in short training sessions of about 10 to 15 minutes a few times a week. As your dog progresses, your children can increase the frequency and duration of training sessions. Regular practice and reinforcement are vital for maintaining and refining these behaviors.

CREATIVE TRICKSTER

Category: Kids games

Objectives

Creative Trickster aims to enhance creativity, problem-solving skills, and the bond between children and their dogs. This exercise encourages children to come up with their unique tricks and behaviors, fostering their imagination and innovation. By engaging in Creative Trickster, children will develop their communication skills, boost their confidence, and deepen their connection with their furry pets.

Description

Creative Trickster is an intermediate-level exercise that empowers children to invent and teach their dogs new and exciting tricks. It encourages children to think creatively and use their imaginations to develop unique behaviors that showcase their dog's talents. This mentally-stimulating exercise promotes collaboration between the child and the dog, allowing them to explore their creativity together.

How to Perform

1. **Brainstorm ideas:** Sit down with your children and brainstorm different trick ideas they would like to teach the dog. Encourage them to think outside the box and be creative. The tricks can range from simple actions to a few complex activities.
2. **Choose tricks:** Select a few tricks from the brainstorming session that are suitable for the children's skill level and the dog's capabilities. Ensure that the tricks are safe, doable, and appropriate for the ages of both parties.
3. **Break It down:** Break down each trick into smaller, simpler steps. Help your children identify the key components of the trick and determine the order in which they need to be taught.
4. **Teach step by step:** Guide the kids through each step of teaching the trick to the dog. Emphasize the importance of patience, consistency, and positive reinforcement. Encourage your children to use clear verbal cues and hand signals to communicate with the dog effectively.
5. **Practice and refine:** Practice each step of the trick with the dog, ensuring that each child provides consistent reinforcement and praise for successful attempts. Repeat the steps regularly to help the dog understand and execute the trick effectively.
6. **Polish the performance:** Once your dog has learned the trick, work with your kids to refine and improve the performance. Encourage them to add flair, creativity, and personal touches to make the trick unique and impressive.
7. **Showcase the tricks:** Provide opportunities for the kids to showcase their dog's tricks to family, friends, or even in dog-friendly events. Celebrate their creativity and applaud their hard work. This will boost their confidence and strengthen the child's bond with the dog.

Recommended Repetitions

Practice Creative Trickster for about 10 to 15 minutes per session; a few times a week is okay. Consistency and regular practice are key to reinforcing the tricks and ensuring that the children and the dog maintain their connection and progress.

CULINARY CONUNDRUM

Category: Food games

Objectives

Culinary Conundrum engages your dog's senses, stimulates his problem-solving abilities, and provides a fun and rewarding experience. This exercise encourages your dog to use his nose and brain to find hidden treats or solve food-related puzzles. By participating in Culinary Conundrum, your dog will enhance his scenting skills, mental presence, and overall enjoyment of mealtime.

Description

Culinary Conundrum is a food-based game that combines the excitement of a scavenger hunt with the challenge of solving food puzzles. It taps into your dog's natural instinct to search for food and engages his brain in a mentally-stimulating activity. This game can be played indoors or outdoors, depending on your preference and available space.

How to Perform

1. **Hide and seek:** Begin by hiding small treats or pieces of your dog's favorite food around the designated area. Start with easy hiding spots that are visible or easily accessible. Allow your dog to observe the hiding process initially to gain his interest.
2. **Encourage searching:** Release your dog and encourage him to use his sense of smell to locate the hidden treats. Provide verbal cues such as "Find it!" or "Search!" to guide his focus and encourage him to explore his surroundings. Remain patient and let him take his time to search.
3. **Gradually increase difficulty:** As your dog becomes more proficient at finding the hidden treats, it's time to take the difficulty level up a notch. Begin hiding treats in more challenging locations, such as behind objects, under furniture, or in elevated areas that require your dog to use his problem-solving skills.
4. **Introduce food puzzles:** Incorporate food puzzles or interactive toys that require your dog to manipulate or solve puzzles to access his treats. These puzzles engage your dog's cognitive abilities and provide mental stimulation. Suitable puzzles for this exercise include treat-dispensing toys, puzzle feeders, or toys with hidden compartments.
5. **Offer positive reinforcement:** When your dog successfully finds a hidden treat or solves a food puzzle, reward him with praise, affection, or an additional treat. Positive reinforcement encourages him to continue engaging in the activity and reinforces his scenting skills.
6. **Vary the locations:** To keep the game exciting and challenging, vary the locations where you hide treats or set up food puzzles. This ensures that your dog does not rely on memory but continues using his sense of smell and problem-solving abilities to find rewards.
7. **Safety first:** Always supervise your dog during Culinary Conundrum to ensure his safety. Avoid hiding treats in areas that are inaccessible or may pose a risk to your dog. Use treats that are safe for consumption and appropriate for your dog's dietary needs.

Recommended Repetitions

Culinary Conundrum can be practiced for 10 to 15 minutes per session a few times a week. The frequency may be adjusted to suit your dog's interest and energy level. Regular engagement in this food game will provide mental enrichment, strengthen the bond between you and your dog, and make him look forward to an enjoyable mealtime.

BALL POOL TREASURE HUNT

Category: Food games

Objectives

The Ball Pool Treasure Hunt exercise aims to provide mental stimulation and engagement for your dog through a fun and challenging game. By searching for treats hidden within a pool of balls, your dog will exercise his senses, problem-solving abilities, and patience. This activity also promotes a slower eating pace for dogs who tend to gulp their food, while helping them build confidence and overcome frustration in new situations.

Description

This Ball Pool Treasure Hunt activity combines the fun of hide-and-seek with the challenge of retrieving treats from a pool filled with balls. It's a fantastic way to provide mental stimulation and curb the habit of eating very fast in dogs. Plus, it can help dogs build confidence and overcome frustration in new situations.

How to Perform

1. **Set up the ball pool:** Place the plastic kiddie pool in a suitable location, preferably outdoors or in a spacious area indoors. Ensure the pool is clean and free from any sharp objects or hazards.
2. **Fill the pool with balls:** Fill the pool with balls of different colors, creating a playful and enticing environment for your dog.
3. **Sprinkle treats:** Sprinkle kibble or treats on top of the balls, distributing them evenly throughout the pool. This will encourage your dog to search and dig for the hidden rewards.
4. **Introduce your dog:** Bring your dog to the pool and get him excited about the game. Show him the treats and let him see, smell, and anticipate the fun awaiting him.
5. **Start the hunt:** Give your dog a cue like "Find the treasure!" or "Search!" to begin the hunt. Encourage him to explore the pool, using his nose, paws, and body to navigate through the balls and locate the hidden treats.
6. **Adjust difficulty:** If your dog is new to this game or easily overwhelmed, start with a few balls in the pool and gradually increase the number as he becomes more comfortable and confident.
7. **Reward success:** As your dog successfully finds and retrieves treats, praise him enthusiastically and offer additional rewards or verbal cues to reinforce the desired behavior.
8. **Repeat and vary:** Repeat the Ball Pool Treasure Hunt regularly to keep your dog mentally stimulated. You can also add variations by using different types of balls or hiding specific toys or objects for him to find.

Recommended Repetitions

You can engage your dog in the Ball Pool Treasure Hunt exercise once or twice a week. Adjust the frequency based on your dog's energy level and interest.

SNIFF PUZZLE CHALLENGE

Category: Intelligence and Brain games

Objectives

The objective of the Puzzle Box Challenge is to engage your dog's problem-solving skills, stimulate his sense of smell, and provide a mentally-enriching experience. This exercise encourages your dog to use his nose and cognitive abilities to locate hidden treats in various puzzle boxes.

Description

The Puzzle Box Challenge is an interactive and engaging game that involves hiding treats underneath one of several empty shoe boxes or large plastic containers. By utilizing his sense of smell and problem-solving abilities, your dog will be motivated to find the hidden treats, providing mental stimulation and a rewarding experience.

How to Perform

1. **Gather materials:** Collect a number of empty shoe boxes or large plastic containers. Ensure they are clean, safe, and suitable for your dog's size.
2. **Prepare the puzzle boxes:** Take the chosen boxes and hide treats underneath one of them. Ensure the other boxes are empty. Start with a simple setup and gradually increase the difficulty level as your dog becomes more skilled.
3. **Introduce the puzzle boxes:** Bring your dog into the room and let him observe the puzzle boxes without interacting with them. Allow him to sniff and investigate the boxes, generating curiosity and interest.
4. **Command and pbservation:** Give a command word such as "Start" or "Find" to signal the beginning of the game. Encourage your dog to use his sense of smell to find the treat. Observe his behavior and provide positive reinforcement, such as praise or treats, when he approaches or interacts with the correct box.
5. **Increase difficulty:** As your dog becomes more proficient, make the puzzle more challenging. You can place a lid on the box, stack boxes inside one another, or create additional layers of complexity to require more problem-solving skills.
6. **Rotate treats** Vary the type of treats hidden under the boxes to keep the game interesting and prevent predictability. This adds an element of surprise and ensures continued engagement.
7. **Patience and reinforcement:** Be patient with your dog as he learns and adapts to the game. Reward his efforts with treats, praise, and enthusiasm to reinforce his puzzle-solving skills and motivate him to continue playing.

Recommended Repetitions

The Puzzle Box Challenge can be played for several minutes per session, a few times per week. The duration and frequency can be adjusted based on your dog's energy level and attention span. Regularly changing the hiding spots and increasing the difficulty level will provide ongoing mental stimulation and prevent boredom.

JUMPING JACKPOT

Category: Agility games, Focus games

Objectives

The Jumping Jackpot exercise focuses on improving a dog's jumping ability, coordination, and agility. The objectives of this exercise include strengthening his leg muscles, enhancing his jumping techniques, promoting body control, and improving his explosive power.

Description

Jumping Jackpot is an agility game that involves your dog jumping over obstacles at varying heights. While this seems more like a physical activity (by testing his accuracy and speed), it also requires him to maintain focus by following cues. Hence, a perfect blend of physical and mental stimulation exercise.

How to Perform

1. **Set up a jumping area:** Create a designated jumping area using agility equipment such as jumps or hurdles. Ensure the area is spacious and clear of obstacles to enable your dog to jump safely.
2. **Warm up:** Start with a warm-up routine to prepare your dog's muscles for jumping. Light exercises such as jogging or brisk walking help increase blood flow and loosen up his joints.
3. **Begin with low jumps:** Start the exercise with low jumps set at a comfortable height for your dog. Position yourself on the other side of the jump, facing your dog.
4. **Use positive reinforcement:** Use verbal cues such as "Jump" or "Over" to encourage your dog to approach the jump. Also, reward him with a favorite toy or treat when he successfully clears the jump.
5. **Gradually increase the height:** Slowly but surely, your dog's jumping skills will improve, and the lower jumps will become easy-peasy. Gradually increase the height of the jump within appropriate levels—i.e., a height that may be a little bit challenging but agrees with his physical abilities.
6. **Pay attention to your dog's technique:** Focus on your dog's jumping technique and ensure he jumps with his leg tucked and body aligned to achieve maximum efficiency. Also, observe his landing stance to ensure a controlled, balanced landing on all four paws.
7. **Introduce different jump types:** As you progress, incorporate various types of jumps, such as double jumps, spread jumps, tire jumps, etc., to challenge your dog's jumping skills and versatility. Also, test his speed and agility by practicing different jump sequences.
8. **Use verbal cues:** Teach your dog to become familiar with specific commands associated with jumping, such as "Jump" or "Hup." Be consistent in the cues you use to signal to him when to jump, and be clear on your instructions on approaching and finishing the jumps.
9. **Practice timing and coordination:** Develop good timing and coordination between you and your dog. Anticipate his movements and provide cues at the right moment to guide them over the jumps smoothly.

Recommended Repetition

The number of repetitions for Jumping Jackpot depends on your dog's breed, fitness level, and age. Start with a few repetitions per session and gradually increase the number as your dog gets better at it. Take breaks between repetitions to prevent overexertion and monitor your dog's energy levels.

TIRE TANGO

Category: Agility games, Focus games

Objectives

Tire Tango is an engaging agility game that focuses on improving your dog's coordination, balance, and physical fitness. This exercise challenges your dog to navigate through a series of tires in a rhythmic and controlled manner, enhancing his agility skills, body awareness, and overall athleticism. By participating in Tire Tango, your dog will develop better coordination, confidence, and mental focus, while enjoying an exciting and rewarding physical activity.

Description

Tire Tango is an intermediate-level agility game that involves your dog maneuvering through a set of tires in a structured order. This game requires him to carefully step through the tires, maintaining a rhythmic and balanced movement. Tire Tango is not only mentally-stimulating but also provides a great physical workout for your dog.

How to Perform

1. **Set up the tires:** Arrange a series of tires in a designated area, ensuring they are stable and securely positioned. The number of tires can vary based on the space available and your dog's skill level. Start with a few tires initially and gradually increase the complexity by adding more tires as your dog progresses.
2. **Introduce the game:** Bring your dog to the starting point of the tire course and get his attention. Use a calm and exciting tone to motivate his interest. Show him a treat or a toy to make him more eager to participate.
3. **Demonstrate the sequence:** Walk through the tire course yourself, demonstrating the desired pattern of movement. Encourage your dog to observe and follow your lead. Use verbal cues, gestures, or clicker training to reinforce the desired behavior.
4. **Start with one tire:** Begin by having your dog step through a single tire. Encourage him to step into the center of the tire and then step out on the opposite side. Use verbal cues and rewards to reinforce every successful completion of each tire.
5. **Progress to multiple tires:** Once your dog is comfortable with one tire, gradually add more tires to the sequence. Start with two or three tires initially and gradually increase the number as your dog becomes more proficient. Focus on maintaining a consistent rhythm and smooth transitions between tires.
6. **Practice different patterns:** Vary the patterns and configurations of the tire course to challenge your dog's agility and problem-solving skills. Create zigzag patterns, circles, or diagonal lines to add complexity and keep the game interesting.
7. **Use positive reinforcement:** Offer verbal praise, treats, or a favorite toy as a reward for successfully navigating through the tire course. Positive reinforcement encourages your dog's engagement and builds his confidence for even more challenging patterns.

Recommended Repetitions

Engage in Tire Tango for about 10 to 15 minutes per session. However, pay close attention to your dog's energy level and physical abilities to determine whether or not to increase or decrease the duration and frequency. Incorporating Tire Tango into your dog's weekly routine will enhance his coordination, balance, and overall athleticism.

DISTRACTED DISTINCTION

Category: Focus games

Objectives

Distracted Distinction is a focus game that aims to improve your dog's ability to maintain attention and focus even in distracting environments. This exercise enhances mental resilience, impulse control, and overall focus in dogs. By participating in Distracted Distinction, your dog will develop better concentration skills, improved self-control, and the ability to ignore distractions.

Description

Distracted Distinction is an intermediate-level focus game that involves creating controlled scenarios where distractions are present, and your dog must learn to prioritize and respond to your cues. This game is not only mentally stimulating but also reinforces good behavior and impulse control.

How to Perform

1. **Identify distractions:** Begin by identifying distractions that are relevant to your dog's environment. These can include toys, other animals, noises, or objects that typically grab his attention. Gradually introduce distractions that are progressively more challenging as your dog becomes proficient.
2. **Set up the environment:** Create a controlled environment where distractions are present but manageable. Start with a quiet room and gradually increase the level of distractions by adding toys, sounds, or other animals. Use barriers or leashes to ensure safety and control during the exercise.
3. **Establish focus:** Begin the exercise in a quiet and calm state. Get your dog's attention by using his name or a verbal cue. Once he is focused on you, reward him with praise and a treat. Repeat this step several times to establish a foundation of focus.
4. **Introduce distractions:** Introduce a single distraction at a time, such as a toy or a noise. As the distraction is presented, use a verbal cue to redirect your dog's attention back to you. Reward him when he responds appropriately by maintaining focus on you.
5. **Gradually increase difficulty:** Gradually increase the difficulty level as your dog becomes more adept at ignoring distractions. Introduce multiple distractions simultaneously or increase the intensity of the distractions. The goal is to create a realistic, challenging environment that mimics real-life scenarios.
6. **Reinforce impulse control:** Use impulse control exercises during Distracted Distinction. For example, ask your dog to wait before receiving a treat or engaging with a toy. This reinforces his ability to resist immediate gratification and maintain focus on you.
7. **Practice in different environments:** Once your dog is proficient in one environment, gradually introduce the exercise in different locations. This helps generalize his focus skills and prepares him to maintain attention in various real-life situations.

Recommended repetition

Engage in Distracted Distinction for about 10 to 15 minutes per session, 2 or 3 times per week. Adjust the duration and frequency based on your dog's attention span and progress. Regular practice of this exercise will improve his ability to maintain attention, ignore distractions, and respond to your cues.

DIY CANINE OBSTACLE COURSE

Category: Intelligence and brain games, DIY games

Objectives

DIY Canine Obstacle Course aims to challenge your dog's problem-solving abilities, mental acuity, and physical coordination by providing an opportunity for him to navigate a customized obstacle course, requiring him to think strategically, demonstrate agility, and overcome obstacles. By participating in the DIY Canine Obstacle Course, your dog will improve his cognitive skills, mental agility, and overall physical and mental well-being.

Description

The DIY Canine Obstacle Course is a mentally-stimulating and physically engaging exercise that involves setting up an obstacle course specifically tailored to your dog's abilities and skills. This game encourages problem-solving, decision-making, and coordination as your dog navigates through various challenges. The course can be customized to include jumps, tunnels, balance beams, weave poles, and other obstacles that require both mental and physical effort.

How to Perform

1. **Assess your dog's abilities:** Evaluate your dog's physical abilities, coordination skills, and confidence level. Consider his size, age, and any existing physical limitations. This assessment will help you design an obstacle course that is challenging yet safe for your dog.
2. **Select obstacles:** Choose a variety of obstacles that are suitable for your dog's skill level. This can include jumps, tunnels, weave poles, balance beams, and hurdles. You can use items like cones, PVC pipes, and boards to create makeshift obstacles.
3. **Set up the course:** Design a course layout that includes a sequence of obstacles. Create a clear path with designated start and finish points. Ensure there is enough space for your dog to maneuver between obstacles safely.
4. **Introduce one obstacle at a time:** Begin by introducing your dog to one obstacle at a time. Use positive reinforcement, such as treats and praise, to encourage him to approach and interact with the obstacle. Gradually increase the difficulty by adding more obstacles to the course as your dog becomes comfortable and proficient.
5. **Encourage problem-solving:** Each time your dog encounters a new obstacle, encourage him to figure out how to navigate it. Use verbal cues, hand signals, or demonstrations to guide him if needed. Let him take his time and reward all successful attempts.
6. **Practice sequences:** Once your dog is familiar with individual obstacles, start practicing sequences of obstacles. Create different combinations and patterns for your dog to follow. This challenges his memory, decision-making, and ability to navigate the course efficiently.
7. **Vary and advance:** Continually adjust the difficulty level of the course to match your dog's progress. Add height to jumps, increase the complexity of weave poles, or create more challenging balance beam configurations. This keeps the exercise engaging and pushes your dog to further develop his intelligence and coordination.

Recommended Repetitions

Engage in the DIY Canine Obstacle Course for about 10 to 15 minutes per session, 2 or 3 times per week. Adjust the duration and frequency based on your dog's physical condition and progress. Regular practice of this intermediate-level intelligence and brain game will improve his problem-solving abilities, mental agility, and physical coordination.

FROZEN GOODIES

Category: Intelligence and brain games

Objectives

The objectives of the Frozen Goodies game are to provide mental stimulation, promote problem-solving skills, and offer a tasty and refreshing treat for your dog. This game encourages your dog to use his senses and cognitive abilities to access the hidden treats, providing a rewarding and engaging experience.

Description

Frozen Goodies is a stimulating and refreshing game that involves providing your dog with frozen treats. It offers a great way to keep your dog mentally engaged while providing a cool and delicious treat during hot weather or as a fun activity any time of the year.

How to Perform

1. **Select appropriate treats:** Choose dog-friendly treats that are safe for freezing. You can use a variety of options such as small pieces of cooked meat, dog-friendly fruits or vegetables, or specially designed frozen dog treats. Ensure the treats are suitable for your dog's dietary needs and preferences.
2. **Gather the necessary supplies:** Get a few ice cube trays, silicone molds, or small containers that are freezer-safe. These will be used to hold the treats while freezing them.
3. **Fill the containers:** Place the selected treats into the ice cube trays or molds, distributing them evenly. You can use a single type of treat or create a mix of different treats in each section.
4. **Add liquid or broth:** Pour a dog-friendly liquid or broth into each section of the ice cube trays or molds. You can use plain water, low-sodium chicken broth, or other flavors your dog enjoys. The liquid helps to bind the treats together and creates a frozen block.
5. **Freeze the treats:** Place the filled ice cube trays or molds in the freezer and let them freeze completely. This may take a few hours or overnight, depending on the size of the treats and the temperature of your freezer.
6. **Present the frozen goodies:** Once the treats are fully frozen, remove the trays or molds from the freezer. Gently release the frozen treats from the containers and present them to your dog.
7. **Watch the fun unfold:** Give the frozen goodies to your dog and observe his excitement and problem-solving skills as he tries to access the treats. The frozen texture and the challenge of breaking them apart will engage his senses and provide mental stimulation.
8. **Supervise and ensure safety:** While your dog enjoys the frozen goodies, it's essential to supervise him to prevent any potential choking hazards or excessive consumption. Provide the treats in a suitable area that is easy to clean and monitor.

Recommended Repetitions

You can incorporate the Frozen Goodies game into your dog's routine as a regular mental stimulation activity. It can be done once or twice a week, depending on your dog's preferences and the weather conditions. Adjust the frequency and portion sizes of the frozen treats based on your dog's dietary needs and overall health. Always provide fresh water alongside the frozen goodies to keep your dog hydrated.

THE BLANKET RACE

Category: Kids games, Indoors games

Objectives

The objectives of the Blanket Race are to promote physical activity, coordination, and teamwork between kids and dogs. This game provides an opportunity for kids to engage with pets in an exciting and interactive way, encouraging a strong bond and fostering a sense of companionship and fun.

Description

The Blanket Race is a fun and interactive game that involves racing your dog while using blankets or sheets. It's a perfect game for both kids and dogs, providing mental and physical stimulation while strengthening the bond between them.

How to Perform

1. **Prepare the space:** Push the furniture back to create a clear and spacious area in the room. This will provide enough room for running and playing the game. Ensure the space is safe and free from any hazards.
2. **Spread the blankets or sheets:** Take a bunch of old thin blankets or sheets and spread them across the floor. The blankets should cover a considerable area of the room.
3. **Position yourselves:** Stand at one end of the room, holding the blankets or sheets up. Encourage your dog to follow you and enter the space covered by the blankets. Make sure your dog is excited and ready to participate.
4. **Start the race:** On your command, start running towards the opposite end of the room while staying under the covers. Encourage your dog to run alongside you, keeping him engaged and motivated throughout the race. The goal is to reach the other end of the room without coming out from under the covers.
5. **Cheer and celebrate:** Encourage your dog with enthusiastic cheers, praise, and positive reinforcement as you race together. Celebrate and show excitement when you both reach the finish line successfully.
6. **Repeat and add challenges:** Once you've completed the race, you can repeat it multiple times, adding variations and challenges to make it more engaging. For example, you can introduce obstacles or create a time challenge to increase the difficulty level and keep the game exciting for both kids and dogs.

Recommended Repetitions

You can play the Blanket Race as often as you and your dog enjoy it. It can be a regular part of your playtime routine or a special activity to do with your kids. Adjust the frequency and duration of the game based on your dog's energy level and physical abilities, ensuring a safe and enjoyable experience for everyone involved.

SHELL GAME CHALLENGE

Category: Intelligence and brain games, DIY games

Objectives

The Shell Game Challenge is designed to stimulate your dog's problem-solving skills, enhance his cognitive abilities, and provide mental stimulation. This exercise engages his focus and encourages him to use his senses and observation skills to locate the hidden treat. By participating in the Shell Game Challenge, your dog will improve his mental agility, concentration, and overall mental well-being.

Description

The Shell Game Challenge is a fun and interactive brain game that involves hiding a treat under one of three cups (or shells) and shuffling them around. This game tests your dog's ability to track the treat and use his problem-solving skills to choose the correct cup. It provides mental stimulation and engages his sense of smell, sight, and focus.

How to Perform

1. **Gather materials for the game:** Get three cups and some small treats.
2. **Present the materials:** Show your dog the three cups and allow him to sniff and investigate them.
3. **Hide the treat:** Place a treat under one of the cups while your dog watches attentively.
4. **Mix around:** Move the cups around and mix up their positions quickly, ensuring your dog is observing the movements.
5. **Encourage your dog:** Prompt him to find the cup with the treat underneath by pointing or using verbal cues like "Search!"
6. **Observe your dog's behavior:** Pay attention to which cup he chooses.
7. **Reveal the treat:** Lift the cup to reveal the treat if your dog selected the correct one. If he didn't, show him that the treat was under a different cup without scolding or punishing him.
8. **Vary:** Reset the cups, place the treat under a different cup, and shuffle them again. Repeat the game several times to provide additional opportunities for your dog to practice and improve his skills.
9. **Increase difficulty:** As your dog becomes more proficient, you can increase the difficulty by shuffling the cups more quickly, adding more cups, or using opaque cups that make it harder to see the treat.

Recommended Repetitions

The Shell Game Challenge can be played for about 5 to 10 minutes per session, a few times per week. The frequency and duration can be adjusted based on your dog's individual needs and preferences. Regular practice and variety in hiding the treat will keep the game engaging and mentally stimulating for your dog.

SCAVENGER'S DELIGHT

Category: Search and scent games, Hunting and prey-related games

Objectives

The Scavenger's Delight exercise is designed to stimulate your dog's mind, engage his scavenging instincts, and encourage the use of his nose to locate hidden treats. This activity provides mental enrichment and can be adjusted based on your dog's energy level, enthusiasm, and food drive. Additionally, incorporating obedience cues like "Sit" or "Stay" enhances your dog's training while he enjoys the scavenging game.

Description

Scavenger's Delight is an exercise that provides an outlet for dogs to use their brain and hunting instincts to locate treats in the house. By creating a recycling treat tower, you'll engage your dog's brain and tap into his scavenging skills while incorporating obedience training.

How to Perform

1. **Gather materials:** Collect bigger and thicker plastics that are not easily chewable by your dog. Alternatively, use a large box or a paper bag to hold the hidden goodies. Ensure the materials are safe and dog-friendly, preventing accidental ingestion.
2. **Set up the game:** Prepare the recycling treat tower by arranging the plastics or placing the goodies in the box or bag. Start with an easy level of difficulty to build confidence, especially if you have a nervous dog.
3. **Incorporate obedience exercises:** Before starting the game, practice obedience cues such as sit, stay, or other commands. This reinforces your dog's training and additional engagement.
4. **Hide the treats:** Allow your dog to watch as you hide the treats within the recycling treat tower. Ensure the treats are securely placed, making it a bit challenging for your dog to access them directly.
5. **Release and search:** Release your dog to begin the hunt. Use a verbal cue, such as "Find it!" or "Search!" to encourage them to use their nose.
6. **Supervise and support:** Keep a close eye on your dog throughout the game to prevent him from getting frustrated and confused. Offer guidance and support if needed, redirecting his focus to the goal of the exercise.
7. **Progression and safety:** Gradually increase the difficulty level of the hunt as your dog becomes more comfortable and skilled. Always prioritize your dog's safety by using materials that are not easily chewable and supervising the activity closely.

Important Tips

- Use dog-friendly treats suitable for the scavenging game.
- Avoid plastics that can be easily chewed or ingested by your dog to prevent any health hazards.
- Ensure close supervision to prevent frustration and potential chewing on plastics.
- Celebrate and reward your dog's success during the game, reinforcing his positive behavior.

Recommended Repetitions

Play the Scavenger's Delight game for approximately 10 to 15 minutes per session. This game can be incorporated into your dog's daily routine. However, you may vary the duration based on your dog's energy level and attention span.

LAUNDRY BIN TREASURE

Category: Search and scent games

Objectives

The Laundry Bin Treasure Hunt exercise provides an exciting opportunity for your dog to use his scenting abilities and problem-solving skills while engaging in an interactive game. By searching for hidden treats in a laundry bin, your dog will enhance his mental stimulation, focus, and obedience, and improve his capacity to solve problems on his own.

Description

The Laundry Bin Treasure Hunt exercise is an engaging and fun way to play with your dog at home. By utilizing a laundry bin and delectable treats, you'll create a stimulating and rewarding game that taps into your dog's natural instincts and challenges his searching abilities.

How to Perform

1. **Gather materials:** Find a laundry bin or basket that is clean and safe for your dog to interact with. Prepare a selection of small, tasty treats that will serve as the hidden treasures.
2. **Introduce the laundry bin:** Set up the laundry bin in an easily accessible location, ensuring it is stable and won't tip over. Show the laundry bin to your dog and allow him to explore it, becoming familiar with it.
3. **Hide the treasures:** Place a few treats at the bottom of the laundry bin, ensuring they are not visible from the outside. You can also add some treats within the folds or pockets of clothing inside the bin.
4. **Initiate the treasure hunt:** Encourage your dog to approach the laundry bin using a verbal cue such as " Laundry Treats" or "Find the Treats!" Allow him to use his sense of smell and curiosity to search for the hidden treasures.
5. **Reward the discoveries:** As your dog successfully finds a treat, offer praise, excitement, and verbal affirmations. Immediately provide him with the treat as a reward for his accomplishment.
6. **Increase the challenge:** As your dog becomes proficient in finding treats in the laundry bin, you can make the game more challenging. Hide treats in different areas of the bin, use additional layers of clothing, or add scented distractions to enhance the difficulty level.
7. **Maintain supervision:** Always supervise your dog during the exercise to ensure he doesn't chew or ingest any non-edible items from the laundry bin. Promptly remove the treats and secure the laundry bin after the activity to avoid any potential accidents.

Important Tips

- Use small, dog-friendly treats that can fit inside the laundry bin and are safe for consumption.
- Avoid using items with sharp edges or small parts that could pose a risk to your dog.
- Make the exercise enjoyable by praising your dog, using a positive and enthusiastic tone throughout the game.
- Regularly wash and clean the laundry bin to maintain hygiene and safety.

Recommended Repetitions

Engage in the Laundry Bin Treasure exercise for 3 to 5 rounds per session, with a break in between each round. Repeat this exercise 2 or 3 times per week to keep it exciting and maintain your dog's interest. Adjust the number of rounds based on your dog's energy level, attention span, and overall enjoyment. Remember to always end the session on a positive note, celebrating your dog's achievements during the treasure hunt.

MENTAL EXERCISE ADVANCED LEVEL

Welcome to the Advanced Games section of the mental health exercises for dogs! In this section, we will explore a series of advanced-level exercises specifically-designed to challenge your dog's mental abilities and promote his overall well-being.

These exercises go beyond the basics and are tailored to dogs who have already mastered the foundational skills. Advanced mental health exercises for dogs require a higher level of focus, cognitive engagement, and problem-solving abilities, making them an exciting and enriching experience for both you and your beautiful furry pet.

By participating in these advanced games, you will not only provide your dog with mental stimulation but also deepen your bond and continue to support his mental and emotional development. For all of these and more, I'll see you on the inside, where we embark on this journey of advanced mental health exercises, where your dog's cognitive prowess will truly shine!

MUSICAL MAT CHALLENGE

Category: Focus games, Impulse control games

Objectives

The Musical Mat Challenge exercise aims to combine the joy of music and movement with obedience training for your dog. By incorporating commands and rewarding your dog's response, this exercise promotes focus, listening skills, and quick thinking. Additionally, it provides a fun and interactive way to bond with your dog while keeping both of you physically and mentally active.

Description

Get ready to dance, groove, and train with your furry friend in the Musical Mat Challenge exercise. This activity combines the elements of music, movement, and obedience training to create an engaging and rewarding experience for both you and your dog.

How to Play

1. **Set up the mats:** Arrange four or five rugs, mats, or blankets on the floor, ensuring they are spaced out and easily distinguishable from each other. Make sure the mats are secure and won't slip or slide during the exercise.
2. **Play the music:** Choose some of your favorite music with a lively tempo to create a fun and energetic atmosphere. Start playing the music to set the mood for the exercise.
3. **Dance and play:** Begin dancing, moving, and playing with your dog in a playful manner around the mats. Engage in activities that your dog enjoys, such as playful movements, gentle tugs, or encouraging gestures. This part of the exercise is meant to build excitement and create a positive association with the mats and the music.
4. **Stop the music:** Suddenly pause the music, signaling a change in the activity. Immediately issue a command to your dog, such as "Sit!" or "Lay down!" Choose a command that your dog is familiar with and has been trained to respond to.
5. **Dog's response:** Observe your dog's reaction to the command. Once your dog performs the requested action, promptly reward him with a treat to reinforce the desired behavior. Use positive reinforcement, verbal praise, and physical affection to acknowledge your dog's correct response.
6. **Restart the music:** Resume playing the music to initiate the next round of the exercise. Continue dancing, moving, and playing with your dog around the mats.
7. **Repeat and vary:** Repeat steps 4 to 6, intermittently stopping the music, issuing commands, rewarding your dog's responses, and restarting the music. Gradually increase the difficulty by introducing new commands or incorporating longer durations of sitting or laying down on the mats.

Recommended Repetitions

Engage in the Musical Mat Challenge exercise for 10 to 15 minutes per session, depending on your dog's attention span and energy level. Repeat the exercise two to three times per week to maintain consistency and reinforce obedience training.

FIND ME FLIP ME

Category: Search and scent games, Indoor games

Objectives

The Find Me Flip Me exercise is designed to engage your dog's cognitive abilities, enhance his problem-solving skills, and provide mental stimulation. This game stimulates your dog's mind by encouraging him to use his sense of smell and observation to locate hidden treats or toys.

Description

The Find Me Flip Me is an interactive exercise that will test your dog's searching skills and stimulate his problem-solving abilities as he learns to work for his treats.

How to Play

1. **Gather materials:** Collect a variety of small containers with lids, such as plastic cups, small boxes, or reusable food containers. Use dog-friendly treats or toys as rewards for his successes.
2. **Set up the game:** Place a selection of containers upside down on the floor, ensuring they are spread out and easily accessible. This game is best played on hard, wooden floors. It's even better and more challenging if the floor is slippery as it poses a bit more challenge for your dog to use his nose and feet to flip the container to access the treats. Start easy with a few containers based on your dog's skill level and gradually increase the difficulty.
3. **Introduce the "Flip" Cue:** Teach your dog a specific cue, such as "Flip" or "Search," to signal the start of the game. Use a positive and enthusiastic tone to engage your dog and create excitement.
4. **Hide the Treats:** While your dog is distracted or in another room, hide treats or toys under a few selected containers. Vary the number of hidden treats in each round to maintain unpredictability.
5. **Encourage exploration:** Bring your dog into the room and give the "Flip" cue to initiate the game. Encourage your dog to investigate and flip the containers using their nose, paw, or nudging behavior.
6. **Reward Successful Finds:** When your dog successfully flips a container to uncover a treat or toy, provide immediate praise and reward. Use a marker word, such as "Yes!" or "Good job!" to signal his success.
7. **Increase Difficulty:** As your dog becomes more skilled, add extra challenges to the game. For example, stack containers or hide treats in multiple layers to require more effort and problem-solving.
8. **Maintain Engagement and Fun:** Keep the game exciting by using different containers, scents, or textures. Rotate the hiding spots and introduce new elements to stimulate your dog's curiosity.

Important Tips

- Use dog-friendly treats or toys that motivate your dog to engage in the game.
- Always supervise your dog during the activity to ensure his safety.
- Avoid using containers or objects that can be easily chewed or ingested by your dog.
- Adjust the difficulty level based on your dog's progress and abilities.

Recommended Repetitions

Play the Find Me Flip Me game for approximately 10 to 15 minutes per session a few times a week. The duration of this exercise can be adapted to fit your dog's energy level and attention span.

JUNIOR DOG TRAINER CHALLENGE

Category: Kids games

Objectives

The Junior Dog Trainer Challenge is designed to engage children in a fun and educational activity while teaching them the basics of dog training. This exercise promotes responsibility, empathy, and communication skills in children while also providing mental stimulation for the dog. By participating in the Junior Dog Trainer Challenge, children will develop a deeper bond with their dogs and gain a sense of accomplishment as they see their training efforts paying off.

Description

The Junior Dog Trainer Challenge involves children taking on the role of a dog trainer, where they can practice and demonstrate their training skills. It's important to emphasize that adult supervision and guidance should be provided during this exercise to ensure the safety and well-being of both the children and the dog. Children will have the opportunity to teach their dogs basic obedience commands, such as "Sit," "Stay," "Come," and "Lie down," using positive reinforcement techniques.

How to Play

1. **Establish ground rules:** Before beginning the Junior Dog Trainer Challenge, establish clear ground rules for both the children and the dog. Teach the children about positive reinforcement training methods and the importance of using rewards such as treats, praise, or playtime.
2. **Select training commands:** Choose a set of basic training commands suitable for the children's age and experience level. Start with simple commands like "Sit" and "Stay" and gradually progress to more advanced commands if appropriate.
3. **Teach the children:** Provide the children with step-by-step instructions on how to effectively train your dog. Demonstrate the correct hand signals and verbal cues for each command. Encourage the children to use a calm and confident tone when giving commands.
4. **Practice sessions:** Conduct regular training sessions with the kids and the dog. Start in a quiet and familiar environment with minimal distractions. Break down each command into small steps and reward the dog for successfully following the children's instructions.
5. **Gradual Progression:** As the children gain confidence and the dog becomes familiar with the training routine, gradually increase the difficulty level. Introduce distractions, practice in different locations, or work on more advanced commands.
6. **Reinforcement and positive feedback:** Throughout the training process, provide continuous positive reinforcement and feedback to both the children and the dog. Celebrate their successes and encourage them to continue in their training efforts.

Recommended Repetitions

The Junior Dog Trainer Challenge should be practiced in short and focused training sessions, ideally 10-15 minutes per session. The frequency of training sessions can vary depending on the child's age, attention span, and the dog's responsiveness. Aim for at least 2-3 training sessions per week to maintain consistency and reinforce the learned behaviors.

HOT AND COLD

Category: Search and scent games, Focus games

Objectives

The Hot and Cold exercise is designed to enhance your dog's scent detection skills, improve his listening abilities, and strengthen the communication between both. By using verbal cues and vocal tones, this game engages your dog's sense of smell and encourages him to locate a hidden treat or toy. It promotes focus, problem-solving, and active participation in an exciting and rewarding activity.

Description

Hot and Cold is an exciting and interactive game that uses verbal cues and tones to help your dog locate hidden treats or toys. It's a fun treasure hunt that engages your dog's sense of smell and encourages him to use his listening skills. By following your cues and vocal guidance, your dog will search for the hidden treasures while enjoying quality time together.

How to Play

1. **Hide the treats:** Choose a spot to hide treats or toys while your dog isn't looking. Ensure the hiding spot is safe and accessible for your dog.
2. **Explain the game:** Let your dog know that it's time to play a fun search game. Teach him that he needs to rely on his nose and listen for special cues to find the hidden treasures.
3. **Use verbal cues:** Use simple verbal cues and tones to guide your dog during the game. Use a calm tone to indicate he is moving away from the hidden treat ("Colder"). Switch to an excited tone to let him know he is getting closer to the hidden treasures ("Warmer" or "Hotter").
4. **Reward success:** When your dog successfully finds a hidden treasure, show him some excitement and offer a reward, like a treat or playtime with the found toy. Celebrate his accomplishments and reinforce the positive connection between the cues and the rewarding outcome.
5. **Increase difficulty:** Once your dog becomes more experienced, you can make the game more challenging by hiding the treats in trickier spots or increasing the distance between hiding places.

Important Tips

- Always prioritize your dog's safety and well-being during the game.
- Watch his behavior and adjust the difficulty level accordingly.
- Remember to provide plenty of praise, rewards, and affection to keep the game enjoyable and rewarding for your dog.

Recommended Repetitions

To maximize the benefits and enjoyment of the Hot and Cold game, it is recommended to incorporate it into your dog's playtime routine regularly. The frequency and duration can vary based on your dog's energy level and interest in the game. Start with shorter sessions of about 5 to 10 minutes and assess your dog's engagement and enthusiasm. If your dog is having a good time, you can gradually increase the duration up to 15 to 20 minutes per session.

THE TOYS' NAMES

Category: Focus Games, Intelligence and brain games

Objectives

The objectives of The Toys' Names exercise are to teach your dog to recognize and respond to to fetch each toy by name, and improve his focus and responsiveness. By consistently practicing this exercise, you will enhance your dog's ability to pay attention to you and follow commands, leading to better communication and cooperation. It can be a fun way to increase their cognitive abilities.

Description

The Toys' Names game is an engaging exercise that aims to teach dogs to recognize their toys' names.

How to Play

1. **Prepare a selection of toys:** Gather a few toys that are unfamiliar to your dog, such as a plush toy, a rubber ball, and a squeaky toy. Choose toys that are safe and suitable for your dog's size and play preferences. Get into position, sit down facing your dog, who should be in a sitting or lying position on the floor.
2. **Introduce target training with toys:** Place one of the toys in front of your dog, within reach of his snout. When your dog leans towards the toy to sniff it, immediately click or say "Yes!" and reward with a treat. Deliver the treat away from the toy, but close enough to your dog so he can stay in their sitting or lying position. Once your dog finishes eating the treat, he will likely turn his attention back to the toy. Click or say "Yes!" and reward again to encourage curiosity and interaction with the toy.
3. **Assign a name to the first toy:** When your dog consistently targets the toy with his nose, give that toy a name. Say the name just as your dog is leaning towards it, for example, say "Plushy" before he touches the plush toy with his nose. Mark and reward his correct response. Repeat this process multiple times to associate the word with the toy.
4. **Introduce a second toy** (without naming it yet): Once your dog has mastered targeting the first toy, bring in a second toy. Place both toys on the floor in front of your dog. Your dog will likely explore the new toy with his nose, but ignore that behavior for now.
5. **Say the name of the first toy:** For example, say "Plushy," and give your dog a moment to think about it. Mark and treat when your dog touches the first toy.
6. **Increase the complexity:** Gradually increase the difficulty by adding more toys, but continue to focus on targeting the first toy by name.
7. **Name additional toys:** To name a new toy, repeat the process starting with only the new toy in front of your dog. Say the name of the new toy just before he touches it, and mark and reward his correct response. Repeat this several times to associate the name with the new toy.
8. **Repeat:** With practice, you can place multiple named toys on the floor and ask your dog to touch each toy by name.

Recommended Repetitions

Enjoy the process and remember that learning to differentiate between toys by name takes time and repetition. There's no rush! Perform The Toys' Names exercise at least 3 times a week for optimal results. Consistency and repetition are key to reinforcing your dog's name recognition and responsiveness. As your dog becomes more proficient, you can incorporate The Toys' Names exercise into your daily interactions to maintain his skills and reinforce his training.

DISCRIMINATION DELIGHT

Category: Focus games

Objectives

Discrimination Delight aims to improve your dog's discrimination skills and enhance his ability to differentiate between various objects or stimuli. This exercise promotes mental stimulation, attention to detail, and cognitive processing. By participating in Discrimination Delight, your dog will develop better observational skills, improved focus, and the ability to make accurate distinctions.

Description

Discrimination Delight is an advanced-level exercise that involves training your dog to discriminate between objects, scents, or other stimuli based on specific cues or characteristics. This game challenges dogs' cognitive abilities, memory, and attention to detail. Your dog will enhance his problem-solving skills, mental agility, and overall focus by engaging in Discrimination Delight.

How to Play

1. **Select discrimination tasks:** Choose discrimination tasks that are appropriate for your dog's skill level. This can include distinguishing between different objects, scents, textures, or colors. Start with simple discrimination tasks and gradually increase the difficulty as your dog progresses.
2. **Introduce cue and reinforcement:** Give your dog a cue that signals the discrimination task is about to begin. For example, you can use a specific verbal command or a visual cue. When your dog successfully discriminates between the desired stimuli, provide positive reinforcement such as praise, treats, or playtime.
3. **Start with twostimuli:** Begin with two distinct stimuli, such as two different toys or scented objects. Present both stimuli to your dog and encourage him to interact with or indicate the correct one. Use the established cue to initiate the discrimination task and reinforce his correct response.
4. **Expand to multiple stimuli:** As your dog becomes proficient in discriminating between two stimuli, gradually increase the number of stimuli. Introduce additional objects or scents, making sure they are clearly distinguishable from one another. Reinforce his correct responses and provide guidance if needed.
5. **Vary the characteristics:** To further challenge your dog's discrimination skills, vary the characteristics of the stimuli. For example, use objects of similar colors but different shapes or scents with subtle variations. This encourages your dog to pay close attention to the specific cues and make accurate distinctions.
6. **Practice regularly:** Engage in Discrimination Delight regularly to reinforce your dog's discrimination skills. Practice sessions should be short and focused, with a few discrimination tasks per session. Regular and consistent practice will help solidify your dog's ability to discriminate rightly.
7. **Gradually increase difficulty:** Continually increase the difficulty level of discrimination tasks as your dog becomes more proficient. Introduce more complex stimuli, reduce the obvious cues, or increase the time between the presentation of stimuli and their discrimination response. This keeps the exercise challenging and promotes continual improvement.

Recommended Repetitions

Engage in Discrimination Delight for about 10 to 15 minutes per session, 2 or 3 times per week. Adjust the duration and frequency based on your dog's focus and progress. Regular practice of this advanced-level focus game will improve his discrimination skills, cognitive abilities, and attention to detail.

OBSTACLE COURSE MASTERPIECE

Category: Kids games

Objectives

The Obstacle Course Masterpiece is an exciting and engaging activity that challenges children to create and design their own obstacle course for their dog. This exercise encourages creativity, problem-solving, and teamwork while providing mental and physical stimulation for both the children and the dog. By participating in the Obstacle Course Masterpiece, children can develop their leadership skills, enhance their bond with their pets, and foster a sense of accomplishment through the completion of their customized course.

Description

The Obstacle Course Masterpiece invites children to utilize their imagination and construct a unique obstacle course tailored to their dog's abilities. The course can include a variety of obstacles, such as hurdles, tunnels, weave poles, balance beams, and more. Through this exercise, children can exercise their dog's body and mind, promoting agility, coordination, and focus.

How to Play

1. **Plan and Design:** Begin by discussing with the children the different types of obstacles they can incorporate into the course. Encourage them to consider their dog's size, breed, and physical capabilities when selecting and arranging the obstacles. Brainstorm ideas and sketch out a rough blueprint of the obstacle course.
2. **Gather the materials:** Collect the necessary materials and equipment to bring the obstacle course to life. This may include cones, jumps, tunnels, planks, or any other safe and suitable objects that can be used as obstacles. Ensure that all materials are dog-friendly and free from any potential hazards.
3. **Set up the course:** Work together with the children to set up the obstacle course in a safe and spacious area, such as a backyard or a park. Arrange the obstacles according to the planned design, making sure there is enough space between each obstacle for the dog to maneuver comfortably.
4. **Introduce the course to the dog:** Guide the children on how to introduce the obstacle course to their dog. Start with simple, familiar obstacles to build confidence and gradually progress to more challenging ones. Use positive reinforcement techniques, such as treats and praise, to motivate the dog to navigate the course.
5. **Practice and refine:** Encourage the child and the dog to practice the obstacle course regularly. Observe their performance and provide guidance on improving technique and overcoming any difficulties. Celebrate milestones and offer encouragement throughout the training process.
6. **Showcase the masterpiece:** Once the children and the dog have mastered the obstacle course, encourage them to showcase their masterpiece to family and friends. Organize a small event where the children can guide their dog through the course, demonstrating their training achievements and the dog's agility skills.

Recommended Repetitions

The Obstacle Course Masterpiece can be practiced for approximately 15 to -20 minutes per session a few times per week. It's important to consider the dog's energy levels and gradually increase the duration and complexity of the course as they progress. Regular practice and repetition will help strengthen the dog's physical abilities and mental focus while providing the children an enjoyable and rewarding experience.

DOG HELPER

Category: Intelligence and brain games, Focus games

Objectives

The objective of the Dog Helper exercise is to train your dog to perform helpful tasks around the house, promoting his obedience, focus, and problem-solving skills. By assigning him specific chores, you can engage his mind, provide physical activity, and instill a sense of responsibility. This exercise aims to enhance your dog's training, foster his cooperative nature, and make him an integral part of your daily routines.

Description

The Dog Helper exercise involves training your dog to assist with various house chores, turning his natural instincts and capabilities into practical tasks. Dogs are capable of learning and performing helpful actions around the house, which not only provides mental stimulation but also promotes their sense of purpose and strengthens the bond between you and your furry companion. This exercise focuses on teaching your dog specific tasks that contribute to household chores, making him an active participant in maintaining a tidy and organized living space.

How to Play

1. **Identify suitable chores:** Identify household chores that your dog can assist with based on his size, breed, and capabilities. Examples of suitable chores include picking up toys, fetching specific items, closing doors or drawers, retrieving the newspaper or mail, or even turning on/off lights with a touch-sensitive switch.
2. **Introduce the chore and provide clear instructions:** Introduce each chore to your dog using a specific command or cue associated with the task. For example, if the chore is to pick up toys, use a command like "clean up" or "tidy." Use consistent verbal and visual cues to communicate what you expect from your dog.
3. **Break down the chore into steps:** Break down the chore into smaller, manageable steps. Teach your dog each step separately and gradually combine them to complete the entire chore. For example, if the chore is to close a door, start by teaching him to touch the door handle and gradually progress to pushing it closed.
4. **Positive reinforcement and rewards:** Use positive reinforcement techniques to motivate and reward your dog for successfully performing the chore or completing each step correctly. Praise, treats, or a favorite toy can serve as rewards. Make the experience enjoyable and reinforce the desired behavior to encourage his participation.
5. **Practice and repetition:** Dedicate regular practice sessions to work on each chore with your dog. Consistency is vital to reinforce their training and help them master the task. Start with short sessions and gradually increase the duration as your dog becomes more proficient.
6. **Gradually increase difficulty:** Once your dog has mastered the basic steps of a chore, gradually increase the difficulty level. Introduce variations, such as different locations or objects, to challenge their problem-solving abilities and adaptability. Ensure a safe and progressive learning environment for your dog.
7. **Monitor progress and adjust as needed:** Observe your dog's progress and make adjustments to the chore or training approach as necessary. Each dog is unique, and some tasks may be easier or more challenging for them. Tailor the chores to your dog's strengths and provide additional support or guidance if required.
8. **Celebrate achievements:** Celebrate your dog's achievements and acknowledge his efforts. Praise and reward him when he successfully performs a chore or demonstrates improvement. Positive reinforcement and encouragement will reinforce his understanding and motivation to be an active helper around the house.

Note

Ensure that the chores assigned to your dog are safe, appropriate for his age and physical abilities, and align with his training level. Supervise his activities initially and provide guidance when needed. Seek professional guidance from a dog trainer if you require assistance in teaching specific tasks or managing any challenges that may arise during the training process.

Recommended Repetitions

The frequency of practicing the Dog Helper exercise will depend on the complexity of the chores and your dog's learning pace. Incorporate chore-related activities into your daily routines and practice them regularly. Consistent reinforcement and repetition will reinforce your dog's understanding and ensure their ongoing engagement in household tasks. Remember to maintain a balanced routine that includes physical exercise, mental stimulation, and relaxation for your dog's overall well-being.

DISCIPLINE IN DOGGY PARADISE

Category: Impulse control games

Objectives

Discipline in Doggy Paradise is an exercise designed to enhance your dog's impulse control skills, self-discipline, and obedience in distracting and tempting environments. This exercise focuses on teaching your dog to make thoughtful choices, follow commands, and resist impulsive behaviors. By practicing discipline in a stimulating environment, your dog can develop better self-control and become more reliable in various situations.

Description

Discipline in Doggy Paradise involves creating a controlled and stimulating environment where your dog can practice obedience and impulse control amidst distractions. This exercise provides opportunities to reinforce training and reinforce your dog's ability to make conscious choices and resist distractions.

How to Play

1. **Select a stimulating Environment:** Choose a location that offers a variety of distractions, such as a park or a busy street. Ensure that your dog is safely leashed and under your control at all times.
2. **Basic obedience reinforcement:** Start by reinforcing basic obedience commands such as "sit," "stay," "down," and "come." Use positive reinforcement techniques like treats, praise, and petting to reward your dog's correct responses.
3. **Introduce distractions gradually:** Gradually introduce distractions that your dog may find enticing, such as other dogs, people, or interesting scents. Maintain a safe distance initially to minimize the level of difficulty.
4. **Practice impulse control:** Encourage your dog to exhibit self-control by asking him to hold positions like "stay" or "wait" in the presence of distractions. Start with shorter durations and gradually increase the time as your dog becomes more proficient.
5. **Distraction training:** Incorporate specific exercises that require your dog to remain focused and disciplined amidst distractions. For example, ask your dog to maintain eye contact while a ball is rolled nearby or have him hold a "stay" command while someone walks by with a tempting treat.
6. **Reinforce good choices:** Whenever your dog makes the right choices and displays self-control, provide immediate reinforcement such as treats, praise, or playtime. This strengthens the association between disciplined behavior and positive outcomes.
7. **Consistency and gradual progression:** Consistency is essential in developing discipline. Practice regularly in different environments with varying levels of distractions. Gradually increase the difficulty of distractions and the duration of impulse control exercises as your dog becomes more proficient.

Recommended Repetitions

Discipline in Doggy Paradise should be practiced regularly, ideally, a few times per week, to reinforce impulse control skills. Each session can range from 10 to 20 minutes, depending on your dog's attention span and progress. Consistent practice in stimulating environments will help your dog generalize the discipline skills to various real-life scenarios.

THREE CUP TRICK

Category: Intelligence and brain games, Focus games

Objectives

The Three Cup Trick exercise aims to engage your dog's cognitive abilities, observation skills, and decision-making capabilities. By playing this game, your dog will enhance his focus, problem-solving skills, and ability to make accurate choices while searching for hidden treats. This exercise strengthens the parent-dog bond between both of you and provides mental stimulation in an interactive and rewarding way.

Description

Get ready to challenge your dog's detective skills with the Three Cup Trick exercise. Using three colorful cups and tasty treats, you'll create an engaging game that will put your dog's decision-making abilities to the test.

How to Play

1. **Gather materials:** Get three cups of different colors. Ensure the cups are sturdy and dog-safe.
2. **Set up the game:** Place the cups in a row on a flat surface, such as the floor or a table. Select one of the cups and hide a treat underneath it without your dog seeing.
3. **Introduce the cups:** Bring your dog to the designated area and allow him to observe the cups. Use an excited and encouraging tone to keep your dog engaged and interested.
4. **Shuffle the cups:** While your dog watches, shuffle the cups around by swapping positions. Continue shuffling for a few seconds to add an element of challenge and confusion.
5. **Cue the search:** Give your dog a verbal cue, such as "Find it!" or "Choose cup!" Encourage your dog to make a selection by using positive body language and vocal reinforcement.
6. **Observe the choice:** Pay close attention to your dog's actions and movements as they approach a cup. If your dog chooses the cup with the hidden treat, praise him enthusiastically with gentle rubs.
7. **Adjust difficulty:** Vary the placement of the treat among the cups to prevent your dog from relying on a specific cup. Alter the spacing of the cups to increase or decrease the level of difficulty based on your dog's progress.
8. **Positive reinforcement:** Regardless of the outcome, provide patience and support for your dog. If your dog chooses the wrong cup, avoid punishment and calmly encourage him to try again.
9. **Repeat and progress:** Continue playing the Three Cup Trick game, gradually increasing the complexity and speed of cup shuffling. Celebrate your dog's successes and offer rewards such as treats, praise, and playtime.

Important Tips

- Always use safe and dog-friendly treats for the game.
- Monitor your dog closely during the exercise to ensure he does not accidentally ingest any non-edible parts.
- Keep the game exciting and enjoyable by introducing new cup arrangements and varying the treats used.

Recommended Repetition

Play the Three Cup Trick game for approximately 10 to 15 minutes per session, 2 to 3 times a week. Adjust the duration based on your dog's energy level, focus, and interest.

STABILITY BALL PLAYTIME

Category: Balancing games

Objectives

Stability Ball Playtime is a fun and challenging exercise that focuses on improving your dog's balance, core strength, and stability. By engaging in this activity, your dog will develop better body awareness, coordination, and overall physical fitness. Stability Ball Playtime enhances the bond between you and your dog while providing an enjoyable and rewarding experience.

Description

Stability Ball Playtime involves using a stability ball to create a dynamic and interactive play experience for your dog. The unstable surface of the ball requires your dog to engage his core muscles and maintain balance while playing. This exercise provides mental and physical stimulation, helping to keep your dog fit, active, and mentally sharp.

How to Play

1. **Choose the right size ball:** Select a stability ball that is appropriate for your dog's size. The ball should be large enough to comfortably support his body weight when he is sitting or lying on it. Consult with your veterinarian or a professional trainer for guidance on choosing the correct size.
2. **Introduce the ball:** Introduce the stability ball to your dog in a calm and positive environment. Allow him to investigate the ball at his own pace. Encourage him to sniff, paw, or interact with the ball to become familiar with its texture and movement.
3. **Encourage exploration:** Once your dog is comfortable with the stability ball, initiate playtime by rolling the ball gently across the floor. Encourage your dog to follow and interact with the ball using his paws. This helps to engage his balance and coordination.
4. **Teach your dog to sit and stand on the stability ball:** Start by guiding him onto the ball with verbal cues and rewards. Gradually increase the duration he remains on the ball, and reward his balance and stability. Make sure to provide support and supervision to ensure his safety.
5. **Incorporate interactive games:** Use the stability ball to create interactive games that challenge your dog's balance and coordination. For example, you can roll the ball and encourage your dog to chase and catch it. You can also teach him to roll the ball back to you using his nose or paws.
6. **Increase difficulty:** You can increase the difficulty level as your dog becomes more confident and comfortable on the stability ball. Introduce slight movements or gentle rocking of the ball to further challenge his balance and stability. Always monitor your dog's comfort level and adjust the difficulty accordingly.
7. **End playtime session with a reward:** Finish each Stability Ball Playtime session on a positive note by rewarding your dog with praise, treats, or a favorite toy. This reinforces his efforts and creates a positive association with the exercise.

Recommended Repetitions

The repetition and frequency of Stability Ball Playtime depend on how physically active your dog is. You may start with short sessions of 10 to 15 minutes a few times per week. Look for his energy levels to determine what durations and repetitions are okay. Regular practice of this intermediate-level balancing game will improve your dog's balance, core strength, and overall stability.

PRECISION TARGET TRAINING

Category: Focus games

Objectives

Precision Target Training is an exercise designed to improve your dog's focus, concentration, and precision in performing specific tasks. This exercise helps enhance his cognitive abilities, attention to detail, and responsiveness to cues. By engaging in Precision Target Training, your dog will develop better focus and learn to follow instructions with accuracy, which can be beneficial for various activities and commands.

Description

Precision Target Training is a focused exercise that involves teaching your dog to target and interact with specific objects or targets. It aims to refine his precision in performing tasks and following instructions. This exercise can be tailored to different skill levels and can incorporate various target-based activities to keep your dog engaged and challenged.

How to Play

1. **Select target:** Choose a specific target object or spot to serve as the focus of the exercise. This can be a target mat, a touchpad, a designated spot, or any other object you want your dog to interact with.
2. **Introduce the target to him:** Introduce the target object to your dog and encourage him to explore and interact with it. Use positive reinforcement techniques such as treats, praise, or clicker training to associate the target with a positive experience.
3. **Target association:** Teach your dog to associate a specific behavior or action with the target. For example, you can teach him to touch the target with his nose, paw, or any other body part. Use clear and consistent verbal cues or hand signals to indicate the desired action.
4. **Target training progression:** Start with simple exercises, such as asking your dog to touch the target with his nose. Gradually increase the difficulty by introducing new tasks, such as targeting different body parts or performing more complex behaviors while maintaining focus on the target.
5. **Reward and reinforce:** When your dog successfully performs the desired action with the target, provide immediate positive reinforcement. This can include verbal praise, treats, or playtime. Reinforcing correct responses helps strengthen the association between the target and the desired behavior.
6. **Gradual challenges:** As your dog becomes more proficient, introduce challenges to further develop his precision and focus. This can include increasing the distance to the target, adding distractions, or incorporating different target objects or spots.

Recommended Repetition

Precision Target Training can be practiced for 5 to 10 minutes per session, 3 to 5 times per week. Adjust the frequency and duration based on your dog's attention span and progress. Regular practice and consistent reinforcement will help your dog improve their focus, precision, and responsiveness to cues.

DRAWER DELIGHT

Category: Intelligence and brain games, Agility games, DIY games

Objectives

Drawer Delight is designed to teach your dog how to open a drawer to access a hidden reward. This exercise focuses on enhancing your dog's problem-solving skills, promoting cognitive development, and providing a mentally-stimulating experience. By teaching your dog to open drawers, you can engage his natural curiosity and intelligence while strengthening the bond between you and your furry pet.

Description

Drawer Delight is an engaging DIY puzzle exercise that involves teaching your dog how to open a drawer to retrieve a hidden reward. This exercise encourages your dog to use his problem-solving abilities, dexterity, and observational skills. By mastering this skill, your dog will learn to associate the action of opening drawers with finding a rewarding treat.

How to Play

1. **Choose a suitable drawer:** Select a drawer that is easily accessible for your dog and doesn't pose any safety or health risks.
2. **Prepare the reward:** Place a highly desirable treat or toy inside the drawer, making sure it's within your dog's reach.
3. **Introduce the target object:** Encourage your dog to approach the drawer and observe his curiosity. Use positive reinforcement techniques such as praise and treats to create a positive association with the target object.
4. **Teach the "Open" command:** Associate a verbal cue, such as "open" or "find," with the action of opening the drawer. Use a consistent and positive tone when giving the command.
5. **Demonstrate the action:** Show your dog how to open the drawer by using your hand or a paw to pull it open. Repeat the action several times while reinforcing the verbal command.
6. **Guide your dog:** Encourage your dog to mimic the action by gently guiding his paw or nose towards the handle or opening mechanism of the drawer.
7. **Reward success:** When your dog makes progress or successfully opens the drawer, immediately praise and reward him with the hidden treat or toy. Reinforce his accomplishment with positive reinforcement techniques.
8. **Repeat and increase difficulty:** Practice this exercise regularly, gradually increasing the difficulty by using different drawers in various locations. You can also hide the reward in different compartments or wrap it in paper to add an extra challenge.

Important Tips

- If your dog finds it difficult to open the drawer on his own, you may create a knot on the handle of the drawer. You can use a rope or ribbons. This would help him get a better grip at opening the drawer and accessing the treat. Before starting the exercise, you can also reinforce his interest in the rope by playing tug-of-war with him to familiarize him with the "Pull" command.

- Remember to supervise your dog during this exercise to ensure his safety and prevent any unwanted behaviors. With time and practice, your dog will become proficient at opening drawers and enjoy the mental stimulation and rewards it provides.

Recommended Repetitions

Drawer Delight should be practiced in short sessions of about 10 to 15 minutes, a few times per week. The frequency and duration can be adjusted based on your dog's progress and motivation. Consistent practice, patience, and positive reinforcement will help your dog master the skill of opening drawers or trash bins to access rewards.

PAWS TO PEDAL

Category: Intelligence and brain games, Agility games

Objectives

The Paws to Pedal exercise aims to teach your dog how to open a trash bin equipped with a pedal. By learning this skill, your dog can assist in disposing of waste and contribute to a cleaner living environment. This exercise promotes mental stimulation, problem-solving and reinforces the bond between you and your furry friend.

Description

Get ready to train your dog to become a helpful partner in waste management with the Paws to Pedal exercise. Through patient guidance and positive reinforcement, you will teach your dog how to operate a trash bin equipped with a pedal mechanism.

How to Play

1. **Select the trash bin:** Choose a trash bin with a pedal mechanism that is safe and suitable for your dog's size and strength. Ensure the trash bin is securely positioned in a convenient and accessible location.
2. **Familiarize your dog:** Allow your dog to explore and sniff the trash bin, getting him accustomed to its presence and scent. Use a calm and reassuring tone to let your dog know that the trash bin is part of his training.
3. **Introduce the pedal:** Show your dog the pedal mechanism by pressing it with your hand or foot. Encourage your dog to observe the movement of the lid as the pedal is pressed.
4. **Paw Targeting:** Train your dog to target the pedal with his paw. You can do this by using a clicker or a verbal cue such as "Touch" or "Paw." Hold a treat near the pedal and guide your dog's paw towards it. When your dog touches the pedal with his paw, immediately reward him with praise and a treat.
5. **Associating the command:** Introduce a command that signals your dog to press the pedal, such as "Open" or "Trash." Say the command just before guiding your dog's paw to touch the pedal. Repeat this process, gradually reducing your guidance until your dog independently touches the pedal upon hearing the command.
6. **Practice opening the bin:** Place a treat or a small amount of food inside the trash bin. Give the command to "Open" or "Trash," and encourage your dog to press the pedal with his paw. As the lid opens, praise your dog and allow him to retrieve the treat as a reward.
7. **Reinforcement and progression:** Practice the Paws to Pedal exercise regularly to reinforce your dog's understanding and proficiency. Gradually increase the complexity by adding distractions or placing the trash bin in different locations.

Important Tips

- Please note that the bin to be used for this exercise should be specifically made for play only.
- Ensure the trash bin is dog-safe, with no harmful or toxic materials inside.
- Supervise your dog during the training process.
- Always provide positive reinforcement, praise, and rewards for successful pedal pressing.

Recommended Repetitions

Train your dog in short sessions, approximately 5 to 10 minutes, a few times a week. Consistency and patience are key to achieving success in teaching your dog to open the trash bin with his paw.

SCENT DETECTIVE TRAINING

Category: Search and scent games

Objectives

The Scent Detective Training exercise introduces your dog to scent work and teaches him to find specific scents. This exercise will help develop your dog's scenting abilities and, in the process, strengthen the bond between both of you.

Description

This exciting journey of scent detection introduces your dog to different scents and teaches him to locate specific odors. With this exercise, you'll unlock his natural olfactory abilities and provide a rewarding experience for your pet.

It is an advanced game because it is not based on the traditional food scents that trigger our dogs' instincts, but rather on teaching them to utilize their sense of smell in a more sophisticated and less instinct-driven manner.

How to Play

1. **Gather materials:**
   - Any essential oil of your choice (e.g. cypress, birch, tea tree, anise, orange, etc.)
   - Cotton swabs
   - Glass jar (small canning jars work well)
   - Treats for rewards
   - Boxes for hiding scents (optional)
2. **Introduce the scent:** Choose the scent you want your dog to detect. Place a few drops of the scent onto a cotton swab and insert it into the glass jar. Hold the jar in one hand and have treats in the other.
3. **Scent association:** Allow your dog to sniff or nose the jar with the scent. Praise your dog when he shows interest by sniffing or nosing the jar. Bring the treat close to the jar and reward your dog next to the scent source. This helps your dog create a positive association between the reward and the scent.
4. **Use verbal cue:** Introduce a verbal cue, such as "search," when your dog engages with the scent jar consistently. Use the cue just before your dog starts sniffing or nosing the jar. Praise and reward him next to the jar to reinforce the association between the cue, the scent, and the reward.
5. **Box hide game:** Once your dog can confidently identify the scent jar on the floor, you can introduce simple hides in boxes. Place the scented jar inside a box, ensuring it is secure and cannot be accessed directly. Give the cue "Search" and encourage your dog to find the box containing the scent. When your dog indicates the correct box by sniffing or showing interest, praise and reward him.

Important Tips:

- Avoid using scents that may be harmful or irritating to your dog.
- Observe your dog closely during the exercise to ensure his safety.
- Gradually increase the difficulty by using more challenging hiding spots or introducing additional scents if desired.

Recommended Repetitions

Engage in the Scent Detective Training exercise for short sessions of 5 to 10 minutes a few times a week. Adjust the duration based on your dog's focus and interest.

DOOR OPENER

Category: Intelligence and brain games, Agility games

Objectives

The objective of the Door Opener exercise is to teach your dog how to open a door using a rope toy. This activity promotes problem-solving skills, coordination, and enhances the bond between you and your dog. By learning to respond to verbal cues and interact with the rope, your dog develops a useful skill while engaging in a mentally-stimulating task.

Description

Door Opener is a training game that involves teaching your dog to open a door using a rope toy. By introducing him to the rope and gradually guiding him through the process, you can help him develop the ability to open doors in a safe and controlled manner.

How to Play

1. **Choose the right rope toy:** Select a sturdy and dog-safe rope toy that can be easily attached to the door handle. Ensure the rope is thick enough for your dog to grip onto comfortably.
2. **Introduce the rope toy:** Allow your dog to sniff and investigate the rope toy. Let him become familiar with the object by using positive reinforcement, such as treats and praise, to create a positive association.
3. **Teach the "Hold" cue:** Hold the rope toy and encourage your dog to take it in his mouth by using a verbal cue, such as "Hold." When he grasps the rope, reward him with praise and treats. Repeat this step until he consistently holds the rope upon hearing the cue.
4. **Modify the rope's position:** Gradually change the position of the rope by holding it from a different angle. Use the same verbal cue and reward your dog for mouthing and interacting with the rope from the new position. This step helps your dog generalize the behavior and adapt to variations.
5. **Attach the rope to the door handle:** Secure one end of the rope to the door handle, ensuring it is safely attached. Encourage your dog to interact with the rope by using consistent verbal cues, such as "Open." Reward him with praise and treats each time he engages with the rope.
6. **Practice with slightly opened door:** Initially, leave the door slightly opened to make it easier for your dog to understand the task. Encourage him to tug the rope to open the door. When he successfully opens the door, use an enthusiastic verbal tone and reward him with treats. Repeat this step to reinforce the behavior.
7. **Increase the challenge:** Gradually close the door more as your dog becomes more proficient. Encourage him to engage with the rope to open the door, using the verbal cue consistently. Reward his efforts with praise and treats each time he successfully opens the door.
8. **Distance and verbal cue:** Once your dog is proficient with the task, gradually move a few feet away from him. Use the verbal cue without physically guiding him. Allow him to respond solely to the sound of your verbal cue and reward his correct actions.

Note

Always prioritize safety during this exercise. Ensure the rope toy is secure and won't cause any hazards. Monitor your dog's behavior and provide him with breaks if needed. Seek professional guidance if you encounter any challenges or have concerns about your dog's ability to perform this task safely.

Recommended Repetition

The frequency and duration of the Door Opener exercise will depend on your dog's learning pace and progress. Practice short sessions of about 10 to 15 minutes each, several times a day, to maintain engagement and prevent overexertion. Be patient and consistent, gradually increasing the difficulty level as your dog becomes more skilled at opening the door.

TRAINING PROGRAM

In the upcoming pages, I've got a cool training plan for you and your furry friend. It's got 4 weeks of basic level exercises followed by another 4 weeks of intermediate level challenges.
Usually, training programs suggest frequent sessions with your dog, like having three short training sessions each day. But if you're attending training courses, they typically happen once a week, along with exercises for you to continue at home.

Now, here's the deal: **this book and these training programs aren't about turning your dog into a champion or entering competitions.** The main goal is to strengthen the bond between you and your dog, have a blast, and make sure your pup stays mentally stimulated to avoid any negative behavior caused by boredom or lack of positive interaction. So, **how many mental exercise sessions does your pup need?** Well, for your average companion dog, training once or twice a day, three days a week, with 5 to15 minutes intervals should do the trick. That's enough to see some solid results. The whole experience should be positive and stress-free, for both you and your pup.

The idea is to actively engage with your dog three times a week, and on other days, you can set up games or provide stimuli to keep your furry buddy happily occupied, reinforcing the progress you've made together. Now let's talk about the time it takes to see the first results. Like anything worthwhile, it requires dedication and patience. But here's the good news: **within 4 to 5 weeks, you'll definitely start seeing some improvements.** You'll notice your pup developing new skills, better attention, and increased concentration. Remember, every dog is different, and each breed and stage of development has its unique characteristics. So, **feel free to invest more time if needed, take it slower if your dog seems low on energy, or speed things up if you're already rocking great communication and learning.**

Building that special bond, engaging in structured games, and if you're new to dog training, acquiring the necessary skills to teach your pup will demand some effort. But trust me, **the satisfaction will be totally worth it for both of you.**

One thing **you'll notice in the training plan is that exercises often repeat themselves. That's because repetition is key when it comes to learning.** As your dog gets the hang of an exercise and finds it easier, his success will boost your confidence. Eventually, **you can introduce more challenges or small variations** to keep him engaged and solidify the milestones you've reached.

So get ready for some pawsome training sessions and let's have a blast with your furry friend!

A 30-DAY BASIC TRAINING PROGRAM
WEEK 1

DAY 1 ACTIVE TRAINING	10 minutes SNIFF AND SEEK	5 minutes EYE CONTACT MASTERY	
DAY 2 REINFORCEMENT	Prepare a STUFFED KONG	Set a ZEN ZONE TRAINING	5 minutes (optional) SNIFF AND SEEK
DAY 3 ACTIVE TRAINING	5 minutes EYE CONTACT MASTERY	10 minutes HIDDEN TREATS HUNT	
DAY 4 REINFORCEMENT	Prepare a TREAT TOWEL PUZZLE	MINDFULNESS MOMENTS	5 minutes (optional) SNIFF AND SEEK
DAY 5 ACTIVE TRAINING	5 minutes EYE CONTACT MASTERY	5 minutes SNIFF AND SEEK	5 minutes FEATHER FRENZY
DAY 6 REINFORCEMENT	Prepare a STUFFED KONG	Set a SOLO PLAYTIME SURPRISE	10 minutes (optional) HIDDEN TREATS HUNT
DAY 7 REINFORCEMENT	Prepare a CARDBOARD TREAT HUNTER	MINDFULNESS MOMENTS	5 minutes (optional) EYE CONTACT MASTERY

WEEK 2

DAY 1 ACTIVE TRAINING	10 minutes BEAM BALANCE BLISS	5 minutes FEATHER FRENZY	
DAY 2 REINFORCEMENT	Prepare a STUFFED KONG	Set a ZEN ZONE TRAINING	5 minutes (optional) BEAM BALANCE BLISS
DAY 3 ACTIVE TRAINING	10 minutes TICK TRAINING EXTRAVAGANZA	5 minutes EYE CONTACT MASTERY	
DAY 4 REINFORCEMENT	Prepare a TREAT TOWEL PUZZLE	Set a SOLO PLAYTIME SURPRISE	5 minutes (optional) TICK TRAINING EXTRAVAGANZA
DAY 5 REINFORCEMENT	5 minutes PUZZLE FEEDER FRENZY	MINDFULNESS MOMENTS	5 minutes (optional) EYE CONTACT MASTERY
DAY 6 ACTIVE TRAINING	10 minutes TICK TRAINING EXTRAVAGANZA	5 minutes SNIFF AND SEEK	5 minutes BEAM BALANCE BLISS
DAY 7 REINFORCEMENT	Prepare a CARDBOARD TREAT HUNTER	Set a SOLO PLAYTIME SURPRISE	5 minutes (optional) TICK TRAINING EXTRAVAGANZA

WEEK 3

DAY 1 ACTIVE TRAINING	5 minutes NAME RECOGNITION RALLY	5 minutes BEAM BALANCE BLISS	
DAY 2 REINFORCEMENT	Prepare a STUFFED KONG	Set a SOLO PLAYTIME SURPRISE	5 minutes (optional) EYE CONTACT MASTERY
DAY 3 ACTIVE TRAINING	10 minutes HIDDEN TREATS HUNT	5 minutes NAME RECOGNITION RALLY	
DAY 4 ACTIVE TRAINING	Prepare a TREAT TOWEL PUZZLE	MINDFULNESS MOMENTS	5 minutes (optional) SNIFF AND SEEK
DAY 5 REINFORCEMENT	Prepare a PUZZLE FEEDER FRENZY	Set a ZEN ZONE TRAINING	5 minutes (optional) FEATHER FRENZY
DAY 6 ACTIVE TRAINING	5 minutes TICK TRAINING EXTRAVAGANZA	5 minutes NAME RECOGNITION RALLY	5 minutes BEAM BALANCE BLISS
DAY 7 REINFORCEMENT	Prepare a CARDBOARD TREAT HUNTER	Set a SOLO PLAYTIME SURPRISE	5 minutes (optional) EYE CONTACT MASTERY

WEEK 4

DAY 1 ACTIVE TRAINING	10 minutes HIDDEN TREATS HUNT	5 minutes TICK TRAINING EXTRAVAGANZA	
DAY 2 REINFORCEMENT	Prepare a TREAT TOWEL PUZZLE	MINDFULNESS MOMENTS	5 minutes (optional) SNIFF AND SEEK
DAY 3 ACTIVE TRAINING	5 minutes EYE CONTACT MASTERY	10 minutes FEATHER FRENZY	
DAY 4 REINFORCEMENT	Prepare a CARDBOARD TREAT HUNTER	Set a ZEN ZONE TRAINING	5 minutes (optional) BEAM BALANCE BLISS
DAY 5 REINFORCEMENT	Prepare a PUZZLE FEEDER FRENZY	Set a SOLO PLAYTIME SURPRISE	5 minutes (optional) NAME RECOGNITION RALLY
DAY 6 ACTIVE TRAINING	10 minutes BEAM BALANCE BLISS	5 minutes TICK TRAINING EXTRAVAGANZA	
DAY 7 REINFORCEMENT	Prepare a STUFFED KONG	MINDFULNESS MOMENTS	5 minutes (optional) EYE CONTACT MASTERY

A 30-DAY INTERMEDIATE TRAINING PROGRAM

WEEK 1

DAY 1 — ACTIVE TRAINING
- 10 minutes SEEK AND SPEAK
- 5 minutes THE WHICH HAND GAME

DAY 2 — REINFORCEMENT
- Prepare a STUFFED KONG
- Set a ZEN ZONE TRAINING
- 5 minutes (optional) SEEK AND SPEAK

DAY 3 — ACTIVE TRAINING
- 5 minutes THE WHICH HAND GAME
- 10 minutes SHELL GAME CHALLENGE

DAY 4 — REINFORCEMENT
- Prepare a TREAT TOWEL PUZZLE
- MINDFULNESS MOMENTS
- 5 minutes (optional) THE WHICH HAND GAME

DAY 5 — ACTIVE TRAINING
- 5 minutes THE WHICH HAND GAME
- 5 minutes SEEK AND SPEAK
- 5 minutes SHELL GAME CHALLENGE

DAY 6 — REINFORCEMENT
- Prepare a STUFFED KONG
- 5 minutes TIRE TANGO
- 5 minutes (optional) SHELL GAME CHALLENGE

DAY 7 — REINFORCEMENT
- Prepare a CARDBOARD TREAT HUNTER
- Set a SOLO PLAYTIME SURPRISE
- 5 minutes (optional) SEEK AND SPEAK

WEEK 2

DAY 1 — ACTIVE TRAINING
- 10 minutes SPIN THE BOTTLE
- 5 minutes SCAVENGER'S DELIGHT

DAY 2 — REINFORCEMENT
- Prepare a STUFFED KONG
- Set a ZEN ZONE TRAINING
- 5 minutes (optional) SPIN THE BOTTLE

DAY 3 — ACTIVE TRAINING
- 10 minutes FIND ME FLIP ME
- 5 minutes THE WHICH HAND GAME

DAY 4 — REINFORCEMENT
- Prepare a TREAT TOWEL PUZZLE
- 5 minutes TIRE TANGO
- 5 minutes (optional) FIND ME FLIP ME

DAY 5 — REINFORCEMENT
- 5 minutes PUZZLE FEEDER FRENZY
- MINDFULNESS MOMENTS
- 5 minutes (optional) SCAVENGER'S DELIGHT

DAY 6 — ACTIVE TRAINING
- 10 minutes FIND ME FLIP ME
- 5 minutes SEEK AND SPEAK
- 5 minutes SPIN THE BOTTLE

DAY 7 — REINFORCEMENT
- Prepare a CARDBOARD TREAT HUNTER
- Set a SOLO PLAYTIME SURPRISE
- 5 minutes (optional) THE WHICH HAND GAME

WEEK 3

DAY 1
ACTIVE TRAINING
- 10 minutes — DISTRACTED DISTINCTION
- 5 minutes — SPIN THE BOTTLE

DAY 2
REINFORCEMENT
- Prepare a STUFFED KONG
- Set a SOLO PLAYTIME SURPRISE
- 5 minutes (optional) — THE WHICH HAND GAME

DAY 3
ACTIVE TRAINING
- 10 minutes — DISTRACTED DISTINCTION
- 5 minutes — SCAVENGER'S DELIGHT

DAY 4
REINFORCEMENT
- Prepare a TREAT TOWEL PUZZLE
- MINDFULNESS MOMENTS
- 5 minutes (optional) — SEEK AND SPEAK

DAY 5
REINFORCEMENT
- Prepare a PUZZLE FEEDER FRENZY
- Set a ZEN ZONE TRAINING
- 5 minutes (optional) — SPIN THE BOTTLE

DAY 6
ACTIVE TRAINING
- 5 minutes — FIND ME FLIP ME
- 5 minutes — DISTRACTED DISTINCTION
- 5 minutes — SCAVENGER'S DELIGHT

DAY 7
REINFORCEMENT
- Prepare a CARDBOARD TREAT HUNTER
- 5 minutes — TIRE TANGO
- 5 minutes (optional) — THE WHICH HAND GAME

WEEK 4

DAY 1
ACTIVE TRAINING
- 5 minutes — SHELL GAME CHALLENGE
- 5 minutes — FIND ME FLIP ME
- 5 minutes — DISTRACTED DISTINCTION

DAY 2
REINFORCEMENT
- Prepare a TREAT TOWEL PUZZLE
- MINDFULNESS MOMENTS
- 5 minutes (optional) — SEEK AND SPEAK

DAY 3
ACTIVE TRAINING
- 5 minutes — THE WHICH HAND GAME
- 10 minutes — SCAVENGER'S DELIGHT

DAY 4
REINFORCEMENT
- Prepare a CARDBOARD TREAT HUNTER
- 5 minutes — TIRE TANGO
- 5 minutes (optional) — SPIN THE BOTTLE

DAY 5
REINFORCEMENT
- Prepare a PUZZLE FEEDER FRENZY
- Set a SOLO PLAYTIME SURPRISE
- 5 minutes (optional) — DISTRACTED DISTINCTION

DAY 6
ACTIVE TRAINING
- 5 minutes — SPIN THE BOTTLE
- 10 minutes — FIND ME FLIP ME

DAY 7
REINFORCEMENT
- Prepare a STUFFED KONG
- Set a ZEN ZONE TRAINING
- 5 minutes (optional) — THE WHICH HAND GAME

DOWNLOAD YOUR GIFT NOW

To download your bonus scan the **QR CODE** below

BONUS

HOMEMADE HEALTHY DOG TREATS

SCAN ME or
http://bit.ly/BONUS_Mental_Exercise_Dogs

LEAVE A SUPER QUICK REVIEW ON AMAZON.COM

Made in the USA
Las Vegas, NV
12 October 2023